SRA Reading Mastery Plus

Spelling Book

Level 1

Siegfried Engelmann
Elaine C. Bruner

A Division of The McGraw·Hill Companies

Columbus, Ohio

www.sra4kids.com

SRA/McGraw-Hill

*A Division of The **McGraw·Hill** Companies*

Send all inquiries to:
SRA/McGraw-Hill
8787 Orion Place
Columbus, OH 43240-4027

Printed in the United States of America.

ISBN 0-07-569027-6

6 7 8 9 MAZ 06

Table of Contents

Note: Begin spelling activities after the first reading lesson.

Introduction

There are 160 lessons in the *Reading Mastery Plus,* Level 1 spelling book. Each lesson takes approximately 5 to 10 minutes to teach. Begin Spelling lesson 1 after completing Reading lesson 1.

The children need the following skills to begin the spelling lessons:

1. identifying and writing the various sounds such as **m, t, s;**
2. "saying the sounds" in a word;
3. "saying a word fast."

Overview of Skills Taught

The spelling program is designed so that the children spell by sounds rather than by letter names. That is, they say the sounds in a word, then write the word.

(Teachers are sometimes concerned that the children will begin pausing between sounds in their reading if pausing is introduced in the spelling. This response does not usually occur. The work with spelling facilitates the children's performance in reading.)

Beginning with lesson 1, the children review saying the sounds in regularly spelled words. These words are presented orally. The children say the sounds in a word without pausing between the sounds. Next, the teacher demonstrates how to say the sounds the "hard way," which involves saying the sounds with pauses between them. Finally, the children write the word.

In lesson 12, the children are introduced to a review format. The words that appear in this format are words that have appeared frequently in the preceding lessons, or are new, easy, regular words. This format does not call for the children to say the sounds in a word before writing it. The children are instructed to "think about the sounds in _____ and write the word."

At Spelling lesson 24, the children start spelling words that are slightly irregular, such as **is** and **has.**

At Spelling lesson 70, the children begin spelling irregular words such as **was.** In the introductory format, the teacher presents a variation of the irregular format used in reading: "When you write the word **was,** you write these sounds: **www aaa sss.**" The children say the sounds. Then they write the word.

After an irregular word has appeared in the introductory format for one or two lessons, it appears in an abbreviated format in which the children say the sounds for the word (without a teacher demonstration) and then write the word.

At Spelling lesson 73, the children start writing an entire sentence from dictation. The children are responsible for remembering how to spell each of the words the right way. The children write one sentence during each lesson until lesson 118, at which time two sentences are introduced in each lesson. The children begin writing three sentences at lesson 154.

The words used in sentence writing have been presented frequently and must have appeared in the review format. The teacher says the sentence the children are to write. The children repeat the sentence. Then they say it the slow way (with a pause between the words). After that, they write the sentence.

Beginning with lesson 77, the children write sound combinations from dictation. The first sound combinations introduced are **ar** and **th.** Other combinations introduced in the program are **sh, ing, al, wh, er,** and **ck.** Note that **ar** is a spelling sound combination before it becomes a reading sound combination (at lesson 106).

Beginning at lesson 95, the children write words that contain the sound combination **th.** The teacher writes words containing the sound combination **th** on the board. The children first read these words and say the sounds for each of the words. After the teacher erases the board, the children write the words.

General Procedures

Give each child lined paper and a pencil. Each lesson takes only a few lines; you may want to collect the papers and pass them out daily until the page is filled.

The children write dictated words in a column (one word below the next).

Depending on the performance of the group, you may be able to teach more than one spelling lesson per day. The criterion for accelerating is that the children achieve 100% mastery.

Use audible signals such as a tap or clap or snap when children are looking at their papers and when presenting series (of sounds or words).

Important Information

1. The spelling program does not rely on joined letters or macrons (long lines over long vowels). Children are not to write either joined letters or macrons. Children also do not write capital letters.

2. If an **e** appears on the end of a word, call the sound **ēēē** when sounding out the word (not **eee** as in **end**). Spelling by letter names comes easier to the children if they are used to referring to the **e**'s on the end of words by the letter name.

3. If a double letter appears in a spelling word, call out the second letter when sounding out the word: **www iii lll lll.** (This differs from sounding out of reading words.)

4. If a vowel in a word is long (the name of a vowel letter), say the long vowel sound when sounding out the word.

Examples:

The **o** in **over** would be **ōōō** (since it is pronounced long in the word).

The first **e** in **ever** would be **eee** (since it is not pronounced long in the word).

The **o** in **not** would be short: **ooo**.

The **o** in **no** would be long: **ōōō**.

General Correction Procedures

If the children make mistakes, follow the correction procedure of (1) model and (2) test.

If you ask the children to say the sounds in the word **man,** and they make mistakes:

1. (Model) Here are the sounds in **man.** Listen. **Mmm** (pause) **aaa** (pause) **nnn.**

2. (Test) Your turn. Say the sounds in **man.** (Signal for each sound as children say) *mmm* (pause) *aaa* (pause) *nnn.*

If a child makes a mistake when you ask the children to think about the sounds in the word **stop** and write the word:

1. (Model) Here are the sounds in the word **stop.** Listen. **Sss** (pause) **t** (pause) **ooo** (pause) **p.**

2. (Test) Your turn. Say the sounds in **stop.** (Signal for each sound as the children say) *sss* (pause) *t* (pause) *ooo* (pause) *p.*

3. (Delayed test) Think about the sounds in (pause) **stop** and write the word. ✓

Note: When signaling children to respond to a sound-out series, use audible signals: (Tap.) *sss* (Pause. Tap.) *t* (Pause. Tap.) *ooo* (Pause. Tap.) *p.*

Summary of Skills Taught

At the end of the spelling program, the children can spell regular words and some irregular words by sounds, and they can write the words accurately. They can spell by sounds words that contain common sound combinations, such as **ar, al, sh, th,** and **wh.** They can accurately spell the words in a variety of simple sentence forms, including questions and some fairly long statements.

Lesson 1

WORD WRITING

Children write **it**

a. Everybody, get ready to say the sounds in (pause) **it.** Get ready. (Signal for each sound as the children say *iiit.*)
b. Let's do it the hard way. My turn. Saying the sounds in (pause) **it. iii** (pause) **t.** I said the sounds the hard way.
c. Do it with me. Saying the sounds in (pause) **it** the hard way. Get ready. (Signal for each sound as you and the children say) *iii* (pause) *t.* (Repeat until firm.)
d. Your turn. All by yourselves. Saying the sounds in (pause) **it** the hard way. (Signal for each sound as the children say) *iii* (pause) *t.* (The children are to pause between the sounds.) Good.
e. Again. Saying the sounds in (pause) **it** the hard way. Get ready. (Signal for each sound as the children say) *iii* (pause) *t.* (The children are to pause between the sounds.)
f. Everybody, write the sounds in (pause) **it.** ✓
You wrote the word (pause) **it.** What word did you write? (Signal). *It.*

Children write **at**

a. Everybody, get ready to say the sounds in (pause) **at.** Get ready. (Signal for each sound as the children say *aaat.*)
b. Let's do it the hard way. My turn. Saying the sounds in (pause) **at. Aaa** (pause) **t.** I said the sounds the hard way.
c. Do it with me. Saying the sounds in (pause) **at** the hard way. Get ready. (Signal for each sound as you and the children say) **aaa** (pause) **t.** (Repeat until firm.)
d. Your turn. All by yourselves. Saying the sounds in (pause) **at** the hard way. Get ready. (Signal for each sound as the children say) *aaa* (pause) *t.* (The children are to pause between the sounds.) Good.
e. Again. Saying the sounds in (pause) **at** the hard way. Get ready. (Signal for each sound as the children say) *aaa* (pause) *t.* (The children are to pause between the sounds.)
f. Everybody, write the sounds in (pause) **at.** ✓
You wrote the word (pause) **at.** What word did you write? (Signal). *At.*

END OF SPELLING LESSON 1

Lesson 2

WORD WRITING

Children write **an, in**

a. Everybody, get ready to say the sounds in (pause) **an.** Get ready. (Signal for each sound as the children say *aaannn.*)
b. Let's do it the hard way. My turn. Saying the sounds in (pause) **an. Aaa** (pause) **nnn.** I said the sounds the hard way.
c. Do it with me. Saying the sounds in (pause) **an** the hard way. Get ready. (Signal for each sound as you and the children say) *aaa* (pause) *nnn.* (Repeat until firm.)
d. Your turn. All by yourselves. Saying the sounds in (pause) **an** the hard way. Get ready. (Signal for each sound as the children say) *aaa* (pause) *nnn.* (The children are to pause between the sounds.) Good.
e. Again. Saying the sounds in (pause) **an** the hard way. Get ready. (Signal for each sound as the children say) *aaa* (pause) *nnn.* (The children are to pause between the sounds.)
f. Everybody, write the sounds in (pause) **an.** ✓
You wrote the word (pause) **an.** What word did you write? (Signal). *An.*
g. (Repeat *a* through *f* for **in.**)

EXERCISE 2

Children write **it, at**

a. Everybody, get ready to say the sounds in (pause) **it.** Get ready. (Signal for each sound as the children say *iiit.*)

b. Let's do it the hard way. My turn. Saying the sounds in (pause) **it. iii** (pause) **t.** I said the sounds the hard way.

c. Do it with me. Saying the sounds in (pause) **it** the hard way. Get ready. (Signal for each sound as you and the children say) *iii* (pause) *t.* (Repeat until firm.)

d. Your turn. All by yourselves. Saying the sounds in (pause) **it** the hard way. Get ready. (Signal for each sound as the children say) *iii* (pause) *t.* (The children are to pause between the sounds.) Good.

e. Again. Saying the sounds in (pause) **it** the hard way. Get ready. (Signal for each sound as the children say) *iii* (pause) *t.* (The children are to pause between the sounds.)

f. Everybody, write the sounds in (pause) **it.** ✓ You wrote the word (pause) **it.** What word did you write? (Signal). *It.*

g. (Repeat a through f for **at.**)

END OF SPELLING LESSON 2

Lesson 3

WORD WRITING

EXERCISE 1

Children write **sat**

a. You're going to write the word (pause) **sat.** First you're going to say the sounds. Then you're going to write the word.

b. Saying the sounds in (pause) **sat.** Get ready. (Signal for each sound as the children say *sssaaat.*)

c. Now you're going to say the sounds the hard way. Saying the sounds in (pause) **sat.** Get ready. (Signal for each sound as the children say) *sss* (pause) *aaa* (pause) *t.* (The children are to pause between the sounds.)

d. (Repeat c until firm.)

e. Everybody write the word (pause) **sat.** ✓ What word did you write? (Signal.) *Sat.*

EXERCISE 2

Children write **in, an**

a. You're going to write the word (pause) **in.** First you're going to say the sounds. Then you're going to write the word.

b. Saying the sounds in (pause) **in.** Get ready. (Signal for each sound as the children say *iiinnn.*)

c. Now you're going to say the sounds the hard way. Saying the sounds in (pause) **in.** Get ready. (Signal for each sound as the children say) *iii* (pause) *nnn.* (The children are to pause between the sounds.)

d. (Repeat c until firm.)

e. Everybody write the word (pause) **in.** ✓ What word did you write? (Signal). *In.*

f. (Repeat a through e for **an.**)

END OF SPELLING LESSON 3

Lesson 4

WORD WRITING

EXERCISE 1

Children write **fin, sat, rat, an, in**

a. You're going to write the word (pause) **fin.** First you're going to say the sounds. Then you're going to write the word.

b. Saying the sounds in (pause) **fin.** Get ready. (Signal for each sound as the children say *fffiiinnn.*)

c. Now you're going to say the sounds the hard way. Saying the sounds in (pause) **fin.** Get ready. (Signal for each sound as the children say) *fff* (pause) *iii* (pause) *nnn.* (The children are to pause between the sounds.)

d. (Repeat c until firm.)

e. Everybody, write the word (pause) **fin.** ✓
   What word did you write? (Signal.) *Fin.*
f. (Repeat *a* through *e* for **sat, rat, an, in.**)

END OF SPELLING LESSON 4

Lesson 5

WORD WRITING

EXERCISE 1

Children write **am, it, rat**

a. You're going to write the word (pause) **am.** First you're going to say the sounds. Then you're going to write the word.
b. Saying the sounds in (pause) **am.** Get ready. (Signal for each sound as the children say *aaammm.*)
c. Now you're going to say the sounds the hard way. Saying the sounds in (pause) **am.** Get ready. (Signal for each sound as the children say) *aaa* (pause) *mmm.* (The children are to pause between the sounds.)
d. (Repeat *c* until firm.)
e. Everybody, write the word (pause) **am.** ✓
   What word did you write? (Signal.) *Am.*
f. (Repeat *a* through *e* for **it, rat.**)

END OF SPELLING LESSON 5

Lesson 6

WORD WRITING

EXERCISE 1

Children write **if, it, sit, sat**

a. You're going to write the word (pause) **if.** First you're going to say the sounds. Then you're going to write the word.
b. Saying the sounds in (pause) **if.** Get ready. (Signal for each sound as the children say *iiifff.*)
c. Now you're going to say the sounds the hard way. Saying the sounds in (pause) **if.** Get ready. (Signal for each sound as the children say) *iii* (pause) *fff.* (The children are to pause between the sounds.)
d. (Repeat *c* until firm.)
e. Everybody, write the word (pause) **if.** ✓
   What word did you write? (Signal.) *If.*
f. (Repeat *a* through *e* for **it, sit, sat.**)

END OF SPELLING LESSON 6

Lesson 7

WORD WRITING

EXERCISE 1

Children write **an, fan, ran**

a. You're going to write the word **an.** Saying the sounds the hard way. Get ready. (Signal for each sound as the children say) *aaa* (pause) *nnn.* (The children are to pause between the sounds. Repeat until firm.)
b. Everybody, write the word (pause) **an.** ✓
c. (Repeat *a* and *b* for **fan, ran.**)

END OF SPELLING LESSON 7

Lesson 8

WORD WRITING

EXERCISE 1

Children write **am, ram, fin**

a. You're going to write the word **am.** Listen. **Am.** Saying the sounds the hard way. Get ready. (Signal for each sound as the children say) *aaa* (pause) *mmm.* (The children are to pause between the sounds. Repeat until firm.)

b. Everybody, write the word (pause) **am.** ✓

c. (Repeat *a* and *b* for **ram, fin.**)

END OF SPELLING LESSON 8

Lesson 9

WORD WRITING

EXERCISE 1

Children write in, fin, an, fan

a. You're going to write the word **in.** Listen. **In.** Saying the sounds the hard way. Get ready. (Signal for each sound as the children say) *iii* (pause) *nnn.* (The children are to pause between the sounds. Repeat until firm.)

b. Everybody, write the word (pause) **in.** ✓

c. (Repeat *a* and *b* for **fin, an, fan.**)

END OF SPELLING LESSON 9

Lesson 10

WORD WRITING

EXERCISE 1

Children write rat, if, it, in

a. You're going to write the word **rat.** Listen. **Rat.** Saying the sounds the hard way. Get ready. (Signal for each sound as the children say) *rrr* (pause) *aaa* (pause) *t.* (The children are to pause between the sounds. Repeat until firm.)

b. Everybody, write the word (pause) **rat.** ✓

c. (Repeat *a* and *b* for **if, it, in.**)

END OF SPELLING LESSON 10

Lesson 11

WORD WRITING

EXERCISE 1

Children write fit, sit, fan, ran

a. You're going to write the word **fit.** Listen. **Fit.** Saying the sounds the hard way. Get ready. (Signal for each sound as the children say) *fff* (pause) *iii* (pause) *t.* (The children are to pause between the sounds. Repeat until firm.)

b. Everybody, write the word (pause) **fit.** ✓

c. (Repeat *a* and *b* for **sit, fan, ran.**)

END OF SPELLING LESSON 11

Lesson 12

WORD WRITING

EXERCISE 1

Children write it, fit

a. You're going to write the word **it.** Think about the sounds in (pause) **it** and write the word. ✓

To correct
1. Say the sounds in **it.** (Signal.) *iiit.*
2. Say the sounds the hard way. (Signal.) *iii* (pause) *t.*
3. Write the word **it.** ✓

b. (Repeat *a* for **fit.**)

EXERCISE 2

Children write at, fat

a. You're going to write the word **at.** Think about the sounds in (pause) **at** and write the word. ✓

b. (Repeat *a* for **fat.**)

END OF SPELLING LESSON 12

Lesson 13

WORD WRITING

EXERCISE 1

Children write in, fin

a. You're going to write the word **in**. Think about the sounds in (pause) **in** and write the word. ✓

> **To correct**
> 1. Say the sounds in **in**. (Signal.) *iiinnn.*
> 2. Say the sounds the hard way. (Signal.) *iii* (pause) *nnn.*
> 3. Write the word **in**. ✓

b. (Repeat *a* for **fin.**)

EXERCISE 2

Children write an, ran

a. You're going to write the word **an**. Think about the sounds in (pause) **an** and write the word. ✓

b. (Repeat *a* for **ran.**)

END OF SPELLING LESSON 13

Lesson 14

WORD WRITING

EXERCISE 1

Children write fan, ran, man

a. You're going to write the word **fan**. Think about the sounds in (pause) **fan** and write the word. ✓

> **To correct**
> 1. Say the sounds in **fan**. (Signal.) *Fffaaannn.*
> 2. Say the sounds the hard way. (Signal.) *Fff* (pause) *aaa* (pause) *nnn.*
> 3. Write the word **fan**. ✓

b. (Repeat *a* for **ran, man.**)

EXERCISE 2

Children write rat

a. Now you're going to write the word **rat**. Listen. **Rat.** Saying the sounds the hard way. Get ready. (Signal for each sound as the children say) *rrr* (pause) *aaa* (pause) *t.* (The children are to pause between sounds. Repeat until firm.)

b. Everybody, write the word (pause) **rat.** ✓

END OF SPELLING LESSON 14

Lesson 15

WORD WRITING

EXERCISE 1

Children write at, mat

a. You're going to write the word **at**. Think about the sounds in (pause) **at** and write the word. ✓

> **To correct**
> 1. Say the sounds in **at**. (Signal.) *Aaat.*
> 2. Say the sounds the hard way. (Signal.) *Aaa* (pause) *t.*
> 3. Write the word **at**. ✓

b. (Repeat *a* for **mat.**)

EXERCISE 2

Children write am, ram

a. You're going to write the word **am**. Think about the sounds in (pause) **am** and write the word. ✓

b. (Repeat *a* for **ram.**)

EXERCISE 3

Children write in

You're going to write the word **in**. Think about the sounds in (pause) **in** and write the word. ✓

END OF SPELLING LESSON 15

Lesson 16

WORD WRITING

EXERCISE 1

Children write if, it

a. You're going to write the word **if.** Think about the sounds in (pause) **if** and write the word. ✓

> **To correct**
> 1. Say the sounds in **if.** (Signal.) *iiifff.*
> 2. Say the sounds the hard way. (Signal.) *iii* (pause) *fff.*
> 3. Write the word **if.** ✓

b. (Repeat *a* for **it.**)

EXERCISE 2

Children write on

a. You're going to write the word **on.** Listen. **On.** Saying the sounds in (pause) **on** the hard way. Get ready. (Signal for each sound as the children say) *ooo* (pause) *nnn.* (The children are to pause between the sounds. Repeat until firm.)

b. Everybody, write the word (pause) **on.** ✓

EXERCISE 3

Children write at

> You're going to write the word **at.** Think about the sounds in (pause) **at** and write the word. ✓

EXERCISE 4

Children write mat, ram

a. You're going to write the word **mat.** Listen. **Mat.** Saying the sounds in (pause) **mat** the hard way. Get ready. (Signal for each sound as the children say) *mmm* (pause) *aaa* (pause) *t.* (The children are to pause between the sounds. Repeat until firm.)

b. Everybody, write the word (pause) **mat.** ✓

c. (Repeat *a* and *b* for **ram.**)

END OF SPELLING LESSON 16

Lesson 17

WORD WRITING

EXERCISE 1

Children write an

> You're going to write the word **an.** Think about the sounds in (pause) **an** and write the word. ✓

> **To correct**
> 1. Say the sounds in **an.** (Signal.) *Aaannn.*
> 2. Say the sounds the hard way. (Signal.) *Aaa* (pause) *nnn.*
> 3. Write the word **an.** ✓

EXERCISE 2

Children write fan, ran

a. You're going to write the word **fan.** Listen. **Fan.** Saying the sounds in (pause) **fan** the hard way. Get ready. (Signal for each sound as the children say) *fff* (pause) *aaa* (pause) *nnn.* (The children are to pause between the sounds. Repeat until firm.)

b. Everybody, write the word (pause) **fan.** ✓

c. (Repeat *a* and *b* for **ran.**)

EXERCISE 3

Children write man, it

a. You're going to write the word **man.** Think about the sounds in (pause) **man** and write the word. ✓

b. (Repeat *a* for **it.**)

EXERCISE 4

Children write **fit, on**

a. You're going to write the word **fit.** Listen. **Fit.** Saying the sounds in (pause) **fit** the hard way. Get ready. (Signal for each sound as the children say) *fff* (pause) *iii* (pause) *t.* (The children are to pause between the sounds. Repeat until firm.)

b. Everybody, write the word (pause) **fit.** ✓

c. (Repeat *a* and *b* for **on.**)

END OF SPELLING LESSON 17

Lesson 18

WORD WRITING

EXERCISE 1

Children write **am, an, ran, fan, man**

a. You're going to write the word **am.** Think about the sounds in (pause) **am** and write the word. ✓

> **To correct**
> 1. Say the sounds in **am.** (Signal.) *Aaammm.*
> 2. Say the sounds the hard way. (Signal.) *Aaa* (pause) *mmm.*
> 3. Write the word **am.** ✓

b. (Repeat *a* for **an, ran, fan, man.**)

EXERCISE 2

Children write **fit, ron**

a. You're going to write the word **fit.** Listen. **Fit.** Saying the sounds in (pause) **fit** the hard way. Get ready. (Signal for each sound as the children say) *fff* (pause) *iii* (pause) *t.* (The children are to pause between the sounds. Repeat until firm.)

b. Everybody, write the word (pause) **fit.** ✓

c. (Repeat *a* and *b* for **ron.**)

END OF SPELLING LESSON 18

Lesson 19

WORD WRITING

EXERCISE 1

Children write **an, man, on, ron**

a. You're going to write the word **an.** Think about the sounds in (pause) **an** and write the word. ✓

> **To correct**
> 1. Say the sounds in **an.** (Signal.) *Aaannn.*
> 2. Say the sounds the hard way. (Signal.) *Aaa* (pause) *nnn.*
> 3. Write the word **an.** ✓

b. (Repeat *a* for **man, on, ron.**)

EXERCISE 2

Children write **mat**

a. You're going to write the word **mat.** Listen. **Mat.** Saying the sounds in (pause) **mat** the hard way. Get ready. (Signal for each sound as the children say) *mmm* (pause) *aaa* (pause) *t.* (The children are to pause between the sounds. Repeat until firm.)

b. Everybody, write the word (pause) **mat.** ✓

EXERCISE 3

Children write **it, fit**

a. You're going to write the word **it.** Think about the sounds in (pause) **it** and write the word. ✓

b. (Repeat *a* for **fit.**)

END OF SPELLING LESSON 19

Lesson 20

WORD WRITING

EXERCISE 1

Children write am, ram, in, fin, on, ron, it, fit

a. You're going to write the word **am.** Think about the sounds in (pause) **am** and write the word. ✓

> **To correct**
> 1. Say the sounds in **am.** (Signal.) *Aaammm.*
> 2. Say the sounds the hard way. (Signal.) *Aaa* (pause) *mmm.*
> 3. Write the word **am.** ✓

b. (Repeat *a* for **ram, in, fin, on, ron, it, fit.**)

END OF SPELLING LESSON 20

Lesson 21

WORD WRITING

EXERCISE 1

Children write in, fin, at, mat, an, man, on, ron

a. You're going to write the word **in.** Think about the sounds in (pause) **in** and write the word. ✓

> **To correct**
> 1. Say the sounds in **in.** (Signal.) *iiinnn.*
> 2. Say the sounds the hard way. (Signal.) *iii* (pause) *nnn.*
> 3. Write the word **in.** ✓

b. (Repeat *a* for **fin, at, mat, an, man, on, ron.**)

END OF SPELLING LESSON 21

Lesson 22

WORD WRITING

EXERCISE 1

Children write it, if, in, on, an, am, at

a. You're going to write the word **it.** Think about the sounds in (pause) **it** and write the word. ✓

> **To correct**
> 1. Say the sounds in **it.** (Signal.) *iiit.*
> 2. Say the sounds the hard way. (Signal.) *iii* (pause) *t.*
> 3. Write the word **it.** ✓

b. (Repeat *a* for **if, in, on, an, am, at.**)

END OF SPELLING LESSON 22

Lesson 23

WORD WRITING

EXERCISE 1

Children write if, it, sit, at, sat, in, sin

a. You're going to write the word **if.** Think about the sounds in (pause) **if** and write the word. ✓

> **To correct**
> 1. Say the sounds in **if.** (Signal.) *iiifff.*
> 2. Say the sounds the hard way. (Signal.) *iii* (pause) *fff.*
> 3. Write the word **if.** ✓

b. (Repeat *a* for **it, sit, at, sat, in, sin.**)

END OF SPELLING LESSON 23

Lesson 24

WORD WRITING

EXERCISE 1

Children write an, am, mat, if, it, in, sin

a. You're going to write the word **an.** Think about the sounds in (pause) **an** and write the word. ✓

b. (Repeat *a* for **am, mat, if, it, in, sin.**)

Children write **is**

a. You're going to write the word (pause) **is.** When you write the word (pause) **is,** you write these sounds. **iii** (pause) **sss.**
b. Say the sounds you write for (pause) **is.** Get ready. (Signal for each sound as the children say) *iii* (pause) *sss.* (The children are to pause between the sounds. Repeat until firm.)
c. Everybody, write the word (pause) **is.** ✓

END OF SPELLING LESSON 24

Lesson 25

WORD WRITING

Children write **am, ram**

a. You're going to write the word **am.** Think about the sounds in (pause) **am** and write the word. ✓

b. (Repeat *a* for **ram.**)

Children write **is**

a. You're going to write the word (pause) **is.** When you write the word (pause) **is,** you write these sounds. **iii** (pause) **sss.**
b. Say the sounds you write for (pause) **is.** Get ready. (Signal for each sound as the children say) *iii* (pause) *sss.* (The children are to pause between the sounds. Repeat until firm.)
c. Everybody, write the word (pause) **is.** ✓

Children write **if, an, on, it, at**

a. You're going to write the word **if.** Think about the sounds in (pause) **if** and write the word. ✓

b. (Repeat *a* for **an, on, it, at.**)

END OF SPELLING LESSON 25

Lesson 26

WORD WRITING

Children write **is**

a. You're going to write the word (pause) **is.** When you write the word (pause) **is,** you write these sounds. **iii** (pause) **sss.**
b. Say the sounds you write for (pause) **is.** Get ready. (Signal for each sound as the children say) *iii* (pause) *sss.* (The children are to pause between the sounds. Repeat until firm.)
c. Everybody, write the word (pause) **is.** ✓

EXERCISE 2

Children write at, sat, it, sit, in, sin, fin

a. You're going to write the word **at.** Think about the sounds in (pause) **at** and write the word. ✓

To correct
1. Say the sounds in **at.** (Signal.) *Aaat.*
2. Say the sounds the hard way. (Signal.) *Aaa* (pause) *t.*
3. Write the word **at.** ✓

b. (Repeat *a* for **sat, it, sit, in, sin, fin.**)

END OF SPELLING LESSON 26

Lesson 27

WORD WRITING

EXERCISE 1

Children write it, sit, fit

a. You're going to write the word **it.** Think about the sounds in (pause) **it** and write the word. ✓

To correct
1. Say the sounds in **it.** (Signal.) *iiit.*
2. Say the sounds the hard way. (Signal.) *iii* (pause) *t.*
3. Write the word **it.** ✓

b. (Repeat *a* for **sit, fit.**)

EXERCISE 2

Children write hit

a. You're going to write the word (pause) **hit.** It rhymes with **it.** This word is tough. I'll say the sounds in (pause) **hit** the hard way. Listen. **H** (pause one second) **iii** (pause one second) **t.**

b. Your turn. Say the sounds in (pause) **hit.** Get ready. (Signal for each sound as the children say) *h* (pause) *iii* (pause) *t.* (The children are to pause between the sounds. Repeat until firm.)

c. Everybody, write the word (pause) **hit.** ✓

EXERCISE 3

Children write at, fat, rat, mat

a. You're going to write the word **at.** Think about the sounds in (pause) **at** and write the word. ✓

b. (Repeat *a* for **fat, rat, mat.**)

EXERCISE 4

Children write hat

a. You're going to write the word (pause) **hat.** It rhymes with **at.** This word is tough. I'll say the sounds in (pause) **hat** the hard way. Listen. **H** (pause) **aaa** (pause) **t.**

b. Your turn. Say the sounds in (pause) **hat.** Get ready. (Signal for each sound as the children say) *h* (pause) *aaa* (pause) *t.* (The children are to pause between the sounds. Repeat until firm.)

c. Everybody, write the word (pause) **hat.** ✓

EXERCISE 5

Children write is

a. You're going to write the word (pause) **is.** When you write the word (pause) **is,** you write these sounds. **iii** (pause) **sss.**

b. Say the sounds you write for (pause) **is.** Get ready. (Signal for each sound as the children say) *iii* (pause) *sss.* (The children are to pause between the sounds. Repeat until firm.)

c. Everybody, write the word (pause) **is.** ✓

END OF SPELLING LESSON 27

Lesson 28

WORD WRITING

EXERCISE 1

Children write am, sam, ram

a. You're going to write the word **am.** Think about the sounds in (pause) **am** and write the word. ✓

> **To correct**
> 1. Say the sounds in **am.** (Signal.) *Aaammm.*
> 2. Say the sounds the hard way. (Signal.) *Aaa* (pause) *mmm.*
> 3. Write the word **am.** ✓

b. (Repeat *a* for **sam, ram.**)

EXERCISE 2

Children write ham

a. You're going to write the word (pause) **ham.** It rhymes with **am.** This word is tough. I'll say the sounds in (pause) **ham** the hard way. Listen. **H** (pause) **aaa** (pause) **mmm.**

b. Your turn. Say the sounds in (pause) **ham.** Get ready. (Signal for each sound as the children say) *h* (pause) *aaa* (pause) *mmm.* (The children are to pause between the sounds. Repeat until firm.)

c. Everybody, write the word (pause) **ham.** ✓

EXERCISE 3

Children write it

You're going to write the word **it.** Think about the sounds in (pause) **it** and write the word. ✓

EXERCISE 4

Children write hit

a. You're going to write the word (pause) **hit.** It rhymes with **it.** This word is tough. I'll say the sounds in (pause) **hit** the hard way. Listen. **H** (pause) **iii** (pause) **t.**

b. Your turn. Say the sounds in (pause) **hit.** Get ready. (Signal for each sound as the children say) *h* (pause) *iii* (pause) *t.* (The children are to pause between the sounds. Repeat until firm.)

c. Everybody, write the word (pause) **hit.** ✓

EXERCISE 5

Children write an, fan, man

a. You're going to write the word **an.** Think about the sounds in (pause) **an** and write the word. ✓

b. (Repeat *a* for **fan, man.**)

EXERCISE 6

Children write is

a. You're going to write the word (pause) **is.** Say the sounds you write for (pause) **is.** Get ready. (Signal for each sound as the children say) *iii* (pause) *sss.* (The children are to pause between the sounds. Repeat until firm.)

b. Everybody, write the word (pause) **is.** ✓

END OF SPELLING LESSON 28

Lesson 29

WORD WRITING

EXERCISE 1

Children write am

You're going to write the word **am.** Think about the sounds in (pause) **am** and write the word. ✓

> **To correct**
> 1. Say the sounds in **am.** (Signal.) *Aaammm.*
> 2. Say the sounds the hard way. (Signal.) *Aaa* (pause) *mmm.*
> 3. Write the word **am.** ✓

EXERCISE 2

Children write **ham**

a. You're going to write the word (pause) **ham.** It rhymes with **am.** This word is tough. I'll say the sounds in (pause) **ham** the hard way. Listen. **H** (pause) **aaa** (pause) **mmm.**

b. Your turn. Say the sounds in (pause) **ham.** Get ready. (Signal for each sound as the children say) *h* (pause) *aaa* (pause) *mmm.* (The children are to pause between the sounds. Repeat until firm.)

c. Everybody, write the word (pause) **ham.** ✓

EXERCISE 3

Children write **it**

You're going to write the word **it.** Think about the sounds in (pause) **it** and write the word. ✓

EXERCISE 4

Children write **hit**

a. Now you're going to write the word (pause) **hit.** It rhymes with **it.** This word is tough. I'll say the sounds in (pause) **hit** the hard way. Listen. **H** (pause) **iii** (pause) **t.**

b. Your turn. Say the sounds in (pause) **hit.** Get ready. (Signal for each sound as the children say) *h* (pause) *iii* (pause) *t.* (The children are to pause between the sounds. Repeat until firm.)

c. Everybody, write the word (pause) **hit.** ✓

EXERCISE 5

Children write **is**

a. Everybody, you're going to write the word (pause) **is.** Say the sounds you write for (pause) **is.** Get ready. (Signal for each sound as the children say) *iii* (pause) *sss.* (The children are to pause between the sounds. Repeat until firm.)

b. Everybody, write the word (pause) **is.** ✓

EXERCISE 6

Children write **his, has**

a. You're going to write the word (pause) **his.** When you write the word (pause) **his,** you write these sounds: **H** (pause) **iii** (pause) **sss.**

b. Say the sounds you write for (pause) **his.** Get ready. (Signal for each sound as the children say) *h* (pause) *iii* (pause) *sss.* (The children are to pause between the sounds. Repeat until firm.)

c. Everybody, write the word (pause) **his.** ✓

d. You're going to write the word (pause) **has.** When you write the word (pause) **has,** you write these sounds: **H** (pause) **aaa** (pause) **sss.**

e. Say the sounds you write for (pause) **has.** (Signal for each sound as the children say) *h* (pause) *aaa* (pause) *sss.* (The children are to pause between the sounds. Repeat until firm.)

f. Everybody, write the word (pause) **has.** ✓

EXERCISE 7

Children write **on**

You're going to write the word **on.** Think about the sounds in (pause) **on** and write the word. ✓

END OF SPELLING LESSON 29

Lesson 30

WORD WRITING

EXERCISE 1

Children write **at**

You're going to write the word **at.** Think about the sounds in (pause) **at** and write the word. ✓

To correct

1. Say the sounds in **at**. (Signal.) *Aaat.*
2. Say the sounds the hard way. (Signal.) *Aaa* (pause) *t.*
3. Write the word **at**. ✓

Children write **hat**

a. You're going to write the word (pause) **hat**. It rhymes with **at**. This word is tough. I'll say the sounds in (pause) **hat** the hard way. Listen. **H** (pause) **aaa** (pause) **t**.

b. Your turn. Say the sounds in (pause) **hat**. Get ready. (Signal for each sound as the children say) *h* (pause) *aaa* (pause) *t.* (The children are to pause between the sounds. Repeat until firm.)

c. Everybody, write the word (pause) **hat**. ✓

Children write **it**

You're going to write the word **it**. Think about the sounds in (pause) **it** and write the word. ✓

Children write **hit**

a. You're going to write the word (pause) **hit**. This word rhymes with **it**. I'll say the sounds in (pause) **hit** the hard way. Listen. **H** (pause) **iii** (pause) **t**.

b. Your turn. Say the sounds in (pause) **hit**. Get ready. (Signal for each sound as the children say) *h* (pause) *iii* (pause) *t.* (The children are to pause between the sounds. Repeat until firm.)

c. Everybody, write the word (pause) **hit**. ✓

Children write **is, his**

a. You're going to write the word (pause) **is**. Say the sounds you write for (pause) **is**. Get ready. (Signal for each sound as the children say) *iii* (pause) *sss.* (The children are to pause between the sounds. Repeat until firm.)

b. Everybody, write the word (pause) **is**. ✓

c. Now, you're going to write the word (pause) **his**. Say the sounds you write for (pause) **his**. Get ready. (Signal for each sound as the children say) *h* (pause) *iii* (pause) *sss.* (The children are to pause between the sounds. Repeat until firm.)

d. Everybody, write the word (pause) **his**. ✓

Children write **has**

a. You're going to write the word (pause) **has**. When you write the word (pause) **has,** you write these sounds. **H** (pause) **aaa** (pause) **sss**.

b. Say the sounds you write for (pause) **has**. Get ready. (Signal for each sound as the children say) *h* (pause) *aaa* (pause) *sss.* (The children are to pause between the sounds. Repeat until firm.)

c. Everybody, write the word (pause) **has**. ✓

Children write **ham**

a. You're going to write the word (pause) **ham**. This word rhymes with **am**. I'll say the sounds in (pause) **ham** the hard way. Listen. **H** (pause) **aaa** (pause) **mmm**.

b. Your turn. Say the sounds in (pause) **ham**. Get ready. (Signal for each sound as the children say) *h* (pause) *aaa* (pause) *mmm.* (The children are to pause between the sounds. Repeat until firm.)

c. Everybody, write the word (pause) **ham**. ✓

END OF SPELLING LESSON 30

Lesson 31

WORD WRITING

EXERCISE 1

Children write **not, rot**

a. You're going to write the word **not.** Listen. **Not.** Saying the sounds in (pause) **not** the hard way. Get ready. (Signal for each sound as the children say) *nnn* (pause) *ooo* (pause) *t.* (The children are to pause between the sounds. Repeat until firm.)

b. Everybody, write the word (pause) **not.** ✓

c. (Repeat *a* and *b* for **rot.**)

EXERCISE 2

Children write **hot**

a. You're going to write the word (pause) **hot.** It rhymes with **not.** This word is tough. I'll say the sounds in (pause) **hot** the hard way. Listen. **H** (pause) **ooo** (pause) **t.**

b. Your turn. Say the sounds in (pause) **hot.** Get ready. (Signal for each sound as the children say) *h* (pause) *ooo* (pause)*t.* (The children are to pause between the sounds. Repeat until firm.)

c. Everybody, write the word (pause) **hot.** ✓

EXERCISE 3

Children write **rat, fat**

a. You're going to write the word **rat.** Think about the sounds in (pause) **rat** and write the word. ✓

> **To correct**
> 1. Say the sounds in **rat.** (Signal.) *Rrraaat.*
> 2. Say the sounds the hard way. (Signal.) *Rrr* (pause) *aaa* (pause) *t.*
> 3. Write the word **rat.** ✓

b. (Repeat *a* for **fat.**)

EXERCISE 4

Children write **hat**

a. You're going to write the word (pause) **hat.** This word rhymes with **at.** I'll say the sounds in (pause) **hat** the hard way. Listen. **H** (pause) **aaa** (pause) **t.**

b. Your turn. Say the sounds in (pause) **hat.** Get ready. (Signal for each sound as the children say) *h* (pause) *aaa* (pause) *t.* (The children are to pause between the sounds. Repeat until firm.)

c. Everybody, write the word (pause) **hat.** ✓

EXERCISE 5

Children write **is, his**

a. You're going to write the word (pause) **is.** Say the sounds you write for (pause) **is.** Get ready. (Signal for each sound as the children say) *iii* (pause) *sss.* (The children are to pause between the sounds. Repeat until firm.)

b. Everybody, write the word (pause) **is.** ✓

c. Now, you're going to write the word (pause) **his.** Say the sounds you write for (pause) **his.** Get ready. (Signal for each sound as the children say) *h* (pause) *iii* (pause) *sss.* (The children are to pause between the sounds. Repeat until firm.)

d. Everybody, write the word (pause) **his.** ✓

END OF SPELLING LESSON 31

Lesson 32

WORD WRITING

EXERCISE 1

Children write **hat, hot**

a. You're going to write the word (pause) **hat.** This word rhymes with **at.** I'll say the sounds in (pause) **hat** the hard way. Listen. **H** (pause) **aaa** (pause) **t.**

b. Your turn. Say the sounds in (pause) **hat.** Get ready. (Signal for each sound as the children say) *h* (pause) *aaa* (pause) *t.* (The children are to pause between the sounds. Repeat until firm.)

c. Everybody, write the word (pause) **hat.** ✓

d. Now, you're going to write the word (pause) **hot.** This word rhymes with **not.** I'll say the sounds in (pause) **hot** the hard way. Listen. **H** (pause) *ooo* (pause) *t.*

e. Your turn. Say the sounds in (pause) **hot.** Get ready. (Signal for each sound as the children say) *h* (pause) *ooo* (pause) *t.* (The children are to pause between the sounds. Repeat until firm.)

f. Everybody, write the word (pause) **hot.** ✓

Children write **hit, ham**

a. You're going to write the word **hit.** Think about the sounds in (pause) **hit** and write the word. ✓

To correct
1. Say the sounds in **hit.** (Signal.) *Hiiit.*
2. Say the sounds the hard way. (Signal.) *H* (pause) *iii* (pause) *t.*
3. Write the word **hit.** ✓

b. (Repeat *a* for **ham.**)

EXERCISE 3

Children write **has**

a. You're going to write the word (pause) **has.** Say the sounds you write for (pause) **has.** Get ready. (Signal for each sound as the children say) *h* (pause) *aaa* (pause) *sss.* (The children are to pause between the sounds. Repeat until firm.)

b. Everybody, write the word (pause) **has.** ✓

EXERCISE 4

Children write **sat, sit, not, rot**

a. You're going to write the word **sat.** Think about the sounds in (pause) **sat** and write the word. ✓

b. (Repeat *a* for **sit, not, rot.**)

END OF SPELLING LESSON 32

Lesson 33

WORD WRITING

EXERCISE 1

Children write **at, is, on, not, if**

a. You're going to write the word **at.** Think about the sounds in (pause) **at** and write the word. ✓

To correct
1. Say the sounds in **at.** (Signal.) *Aaat.*
2. Say the sounds the hard way. (Signal.) *Aaa* (pause) *t.*
3. Write the word **at.** ✓

b. You're going to write the word **is.** Think about the sounds in (pause) **is** and write the word. ✓

To correct
1. Say the sounds the hard way. (Signal.) *iii* (pause) *sss.*
2. Write the word **is.** ✓

c. (Repeat *a* for **on, not, if.**)

EXERCISE 2

Children write **hot**

a. You're going to write the word (pause) **hot.** This word rhymes with **not.** I'll say the sounds in (pause) **hot** the hard way. Listen. **H** (pause) *ooo* (pause) *t.*

b. Your turn. Say the sounds in (pause) **hot.** Get ready. (Signal for each sound as the children say) *h* (pause) *ooo* (pause) *t.* (The children are to pause between the sounds. Repeat until firm.)

c. Everybody, write the word (pause) **hot.** ✓

EXERCISE 3

Children write **rim**

a. You're going to write the word **rim**. Listen. **Rim.** Saying the sounds in (pause) **rim** the hard way. Get ready. (Signal for each sound as the children say) *rrr* (pause) *iii* (pause) *mmm.* (The children are to pause between the sounds. Repeat until firm.)

b. Everybody, write the word (pause) **rim.** ✓

EXERCISE 4

Children write **him**

a. You're going to write the word (pause) **him.** It rhymes with **rim.** This word is tough. I'll say the sounds in (pause) **him** the hard way. Listen **H** (pause) **iii** (pause) **mmm.**

b. Your turn. Say the sounds in (pause) **him.** Get ready. (Signal for each sound as the children say) *h* (pause) *iii* (pause) *mmm.* (The children are to pause between the sounds. Repeat until firm.)

c. Everybody, write the word (pause) **him.** ✓

END OF SPELLING LESSON 33

Lesson 34

WORD WRITING

EXERCISE 1

Children write **sam, ham, not, hot, hit, hat**

a. You're going to write the word **sam.** Think about the sounds in (pause) **sam** and write the word. ✓

> **To correct**
> 1. Say the sounds in **sam.** (Signal.) *Sssaaammm.*
> 2. Say the sounds the hard way. (Signal.) *Sss* (pause) *aaa* (pause) *mmm.*
> 3. Write the word **sam.** ✓

b. (Repeat *a* for **ham, not, hot, hit, hat.**)

EXERCISE 2

Children write **him**

a. You're going to write the word (pause) **him.** This word rhymes with **rim.** I'll say the sounds in (pause) **him** the hard way. Listen. **H** (pause) **iii** (pause) **mmm.**

b. Your turn. Say the sounds in (pause) **him.** Get ready. (Signal for each sound as the children say) *h* (pause) *iii* (pause) *mmm.* (The children are to pause between the sounds. Repeat until firm.)

c. Everybody, write the word (pause) **him.** ✓

EXERCISE 3

Children write **on, if, an, is**

a. You're going to write the word **on.** Think about the sounds in (pause) **on** and write the word. ✓

b. (Repeat *a* for **if, an, is.**)

END OF SPELLING LESSON 34

Lesson 35

WORD WRITING

EXERCISE 1

Children write **him**

a. You're going to write the word (pause) **him.** This word rhymes with **rim.** I'll say the sounds in (pause) **him** the hard way. Listen. **H** (pause) **iii** (pause) **mmm.**

b. Your turn. Say the sounds in (pause) **him.** Get ready. (Signal for each sound as the children say) *h* (pause) *iii* (pause) *mmm.* (The children are to pause between the sounds. Repeat until firm.)

c. Everybody, write the word (pause) **him.** ✓

Children write **sun**

a. You're going to write the word **sun**. Listen. **Sun**. Saying the sounds in (pause) **sun** the hard way. Get ready. (Signal for each sound as the children say) *sss* (pause) *uuu* (pause) *nnn*. (The children are to pause between the sounds. Repeat until firm.)

b. Everybody, write the word (pause) **sun**. ✓

Children write **not**

You're going to write the word **not**. Think about the sounds in (pause) **not** and write the word. ✓

> **To correct**
> 1. Say the sounds in **not**. (Signal.) *Nnnooot.*
> 2. Say the sounds the hard way. (Signal.) *Nnn* (pause) *ooo* (pause) *t*.
> 3. Write the word **not**. ✓

Children write **nut**

a. You're going to write the word **nut**. Listen. **Nut**. Saying the sounds in (pause) **nut** the hard way. Get ready. (Signal for each sound as the children say) *nnn* (pause) *uuu* (pause) *t*. (The children are to pause between the sounds. Repeat until firm.)

b. Everybody, write the word (pause) **nut**. ✓

Children write **ron**

You're going to write the word **ron**. Think about the sounds in (pause) **ron** and write the word. ✓

Children write **run, fun**

a. You're going to write the word **run**. Listen. **Run**. Saying the sounds in (pause) **run** the hard way. Get ready. (Signal for each sound as the children say) *rrr* (pause) *uuu* (pause) *nnn*. (The children are to pause between the sounds. Repeat until firm.)

b. Everybody, write the word (pause) **run**. ✓

c. (Repeat a and b for **fun**.)

Children write **if**

a. You're going to write the word **if**. Think about the sounds in (pause) **if** and write the word. ✓

END OF SPELLING LESSON 35

Lesson 36

WORD WRITING

Children write **fun**

a. You're going to write the word **fun**. Listen. **Fun**. Saying the sounds in (pause) **fun** the hard way. Get ready. (Signal for each sound as the children say) *fff* (pause) *uuu* (pause) *nnn*. (The children are to pause between the sounds. Repeat until firm.)

b. Everybody, write the word (pause) **fun**. ✓

Children write **fin, on, am**

a. You're going to write the word **fin**. Think about the sounds in (pause) **fin** and write the word. ✓

b. (Repeat *a* for **on, am.**)

Children write **his**

a. You're going to write the word (pause) **his.** Say the sounds you write for (pause) **his.** Get ready. (Signal for each sound as the children say) *h* (pause) *iii* (pause) *sss.* (The children are to pause between the sounds. Repeat until firm.)
b. Everybody, write the word (pause) **his.** ✓

Children write **hot**

You're going to write the word **hot.** Think about the sounds in (pause) **hot** and write the word. ✓

Children write **nut**

a. You're going to write the word **nut.** Listen. **Nut.** Saying the sounds in (pause) **nut** the hard way. Get ready. (Signal for each sound as the children say) *nnn* (pause) *uuu* (pause) *t.* (The children are to pause between the sounds. Repeat until firm.)
b. Everybody, write the word (pause) **nut.** ✓

END OF SPELLING LESSON 36

Lesson 37

WORD WRITING

Children write **ran, man, fan**

a. You're going to write the word **ran.** Think about the sounds in (pause) **ran** and write the word. ✓

b. (Repeat *a* for **man, fan.**)

Children write **run**

a. You're going to write the word **run.** Listen. **Run.** Saying the sounds in (pause) **run** the hard way. Get ready. (Signal for each sound as the children say) *rrr* (pause) *uuu* (pause) *nnn.* (The children are to pause between the sounds. Repeat until firm.)
b. Everybody, write the word (pause) **run.** ✓

Children write **sit, sun, hot**

a. You're going to write the word **sit.** Think about the sounds in (pause) **sit** and write the word. ✓
b. (Repeat *a* for **sun, hot.**)

Children write **hut**

a. You're going to write the word **hut.** Listen. **Hut.** Saying the sounds in (pause) **hut** the hard way. Get ready. (Signal for each sound as the children say) *h* (pause) *uuu* (pause) *t.* (The children are to pause between the sounds. Repeat until firm.)
b. Everybody, write the word (pause) **hut.** ✓

EXERCISE 5

Children write **hit**

You're going to write the word **hit.** Think about the sounds in (pause) **hit** and write the word. ✓

END OF SPELLING LESSON 37

Lesson 38

WORD WRITING

EXERCISE 1

Children write **hum**

a. You're going to write the word (pause) **hum.** It rhymes with **gum.** This word is tough. I'll say the sounds in (pause) **hum** the hard way. Listen. **H** (pause) *uuu* (pause) **mmm.**

b. Your turn. Say the sounds in (pause) **hum.** Get ready. (Signal for each sound as the children say) *h* (pause) *uuu* (pause) *mmm.* (The children are to pause between the sounds. Repeat until firm.)

c. Everybody, write the word (pause) **hum.** ✓

EXERCISE 2

Children write **him, ham**

a. You're going to write the word **him.** Think about the sounds in (pause) **him** and write the word. ✓

> **To correct**
> 1. Say the sounds in **him.** (Signal.) *Hiiimmm.*
> 2. Say the sounds the hard way. (Signal.) *H* (pause) *iii* (pause) *mmm.*
> 3. Write the word **him.** ✓

b. (Repeat *a* for **ham.**)

EXERCISE 3

Children write **has**

a. You're going to write the word (pause) **has.** Say the sounds you write for (pause) **has.** Get ready. (Signal for each sound as the children say) *h* (pause) *aaa* (pause) *sss.* (The children are to pause between the sounds. Repeat until firm.)

b. Everybody, write the word (pause) **has.** ✓

EXERCISE 4

Children write **not, nut, rut, on, hot**

a. You're going to write the word **not.** Think about the sounds in (pause) **not** and write the word. ✓

b. (Repeat *a* for **nut, rut, on, hot.**)

END OF SPELLING LESSON 38

Lesson 39

WORD WRITING

EXERCISE 1

Children write **fit, on, rat, his, has, mat, run, sit, not, an**

a. You're going to write the word **fit.** Think about the sounds in (pause) **fit** and write the word. ✓

> **To correct**
> 1. Say the sounds in **fit.** (Signal.) *Fffiiit.*
> 2. Say the sounds the hard way. (Signal.) *Fff* (pause) *iii* (pause) *t.*
> 3. Write the word **fit.** ✓

b. (Repeat *a* for **on, rat.**)

c. You're going to write the word **his.** Think about the sounds in (pause) **his** and write the word. ✓

> **To correct**
> 1. Say the sounds the hard way. (Signal.) *H* (pause) *iii* (pause) *sss.*
> 2. Write the word **his.** ✓

d. (Repeat *c* for **has.**)

e. (Repeat *a* for **mat, run, sit, not, an.**)

END OF SPELLING LESSON 39

Lesson 40

WORD WRITING

EXERCISE 1

Children write fat, run, is, fan, hut, hat, fun, hot, if, on

a. You're going to write the word **fat**. Think about the sounds in (pause) **fat** and write the word. ✓

> **To correct**
> 1. Say the sounds in **fat**. (Signal.) *Fffaaat*.
> 2. Say the sounds the hard way. (Signal.) *Fff* (pause) *aaa* (pause) *t*.
> 3. Write the word **fat**. ✓

b. (Repeat *a* for **run**.)

c. You're going to write the word **is**. Think about the sounds in (pause) **is** and write the word. ✓

> **To correct**
> 1. Say the sounds the hard way. (Signal.) *iii* (pause) *sss*.
> 2. Write the word **is**. ✓

d. (Repeat *a* for **fan, hut, hat, fun, hot, if, on**.)

END OF SPELLING LESSON 40

Lesson 41

WORD WRITING

EXERCISE 1

Children write fun, if, not, run, sit, ran, sat, fan, man, has

a. You're going to write the word **fun**. Think about the sounds in (pause) **fun** and write the word. ✓

> **To correct**
> 1. Say the sounds in **fun**. (Signal.) *Fffuuunnn*.
> 2. Say the sounds the hard way. (Signal.) *Fff* (pause) *uuu* (pause) *nnn*.
> 3. Write the word **fun**. ✓

b. (Repeat *a* for **if, not, run, sit, ran, sat, fan, man**.)

c. You're going to write the word **has**. Think about the sounds in (pause) **has** and write the word. ✓

> **To correct**
> 1. Say the sounds the hard way. (Signal.) *H* (pause) *aaa* (pause) *sss*.
> 2. Write the word **has**. ✓

END OF SPELLING LESSON 41

Lesson 42

WORD WRITING

EXERCISE 1

Children write ham, nut, fat, hot, fun, hit, on, man, if, has

a. You're going to write the word **ham**. Think about the sounds in (pause) **ham** and write the word. ✓

> **To correct**
> 1. Say the sounds in **ham**. (Signal.) *Haaammm*.
> 2. Say the sounds the hard way. (Signal.) *H* (pause) *aaa* (pause) *mmm*.
> 3. Write the word **ham**. ✓

b. (Repeat *a* for **nut, fat, hot, fun, hit, on, man, if**.)

c. You're going to write the word **has**. Think about the sounds in (pause) **has** and write the word. ✓

> **To correct**
> 1. Say the sounds the hard way. (Signal.) *H* (pause) *aaa* (pause) *sss*.
> 2. Write the word **has**. ✓

END OF SPELLING LESSON 42

Lesson 43

WORD WRITING

EXERCISE 1

Children write rat, ran, fit, sun, rut, an, fin, hut, it, fan

a. You're going to write the word **rat.** Think about the sounds in (pause) **rat** and write the word. ✓

> **To correct**
> 1. Say the sounds in **rat.** (Signal.) *Rrraaat.*
> 2. Say the sounds the hard way. (Signal.) *Rrr* (pause) *aaa* (pause) *t.*
> 3. Write the word **rat.** ✓

b. (Repeat *a* for **ran, fit, sun, rut, an, fin, hut, it, fan.**)

END OF SPELLING LESSON 43

Lesson 44

WORD WRITING

EXERCISE 1

Children write him, ham, hot, if, am, hum, not, on, mat, sit

a. You're going to write the word **him.** Think about the sounds in (pause) **him** and write the word. ✓

> **To correct**
> 1. Say the sounds in **him.** (Signal.) *Hiiimmm.*
> 2. Say the sounds the hard way. (Signal.) *H* (pause) *iii* (pause) *mmm.*
> 3. Write the word **him.** ✓

b. (Repeat *a* for **ham, hot, if, am, hum, not, on, mat, sit.**)

END OF SPELLING LESSON 44

Lesson 45

WORD WRITING

EXERCISE 1

Children write is, an, run, mat, in, rut, on, hat, sin, fun

a. You're going to write the word **is.** Think about the sounds in (pause) **is** and write the word. ✓

> **To correct**
> 1. Say the sounds the hard way. (Signal.) *iii* (pause) *sss.*
> 2. Write the word **is.** ✓

b. You're going to write the word **an.** Think about the sounds in (pause) **an** and write the word. ✓

> **To correct**
> 1. Say the sounds in **an.** (Signal.) *Aaannn.*
> 2. Say the sounds the hard way. (Signal.) *Aaa* (pause) *nnn.*
> 3. Write the word **an.** ✓

c. (Repeat *b* for **run, mat, in, rut, on, hat, sin, fun.**)

END OF SPELLING LESSON 45

Lesson 46

WORD WRITING

EXERCISE 1

Children write has, mat

a. You're going to write the word **has.** Think about the sounds in (pause) **has** and write the word. ✓

> **To correct**
> 1. Say the sounds the hard way. (Signal.) *H* (pause) *aaa* (pause) *sss.*
> 2. Write the word **has.** ✓

b. Now you're going to write the word **mat.** Think about the sounds in (pause) **mat** and write the word. ✓

To correct

1. Say the sounds in **mat**. (Signal.) *Mmmaaat.*
2. Say the sounds the hard way. (Signal.) *Mmm* (pause) *aaa* (pause) *t.*
3. Write the word **mat**. ✓

Children write **mad**

a. You're going to write the word **mad**. Listen. **Mad.** Saying the sounds in (pause) **mad** the hard way. Get ready. (Signal for each sound as the children say) *mmm* (pause) *aaa* (pause) *d.* (The children are to pause between the sounds. Repeat until firm.)
b. Everybody, write the word (pause) **mad**. ✓

Children write **if**

You're going to write the word **if**. Think about the sounds in (pause) **if** and write the word. ✓

Children write **sad**

a. You're going to write the word **sad**. Listen. **Sad.** Saying the sounds in (pause) **sad** the hard way. Get ready. (Signal for each sound as the children say) *sss* (pause) *aaa* (pause) *d.* (The children are to pause between the sounds. Repeat until firm.)
b. Everybody, write the word (pause) **sad**. ✓

Children write **had**

a. You're going to write the word (pause) **had**. It rhymes with **sad**. This word is tough. I'll say the sounds in (pause) **had** the hard way. Listen. **H** (pause) *aaa* (pause) **d**.
b. Your turn. Say the sounds in (pause) **had**. Get ready. (Signal for each sound as the children say) *h* (pause) *aaa* (pause) *d*. (The children are to pause between the sounds. Repeat until firm.)
c. Everybody, write the word (pause) **had**. ✓

Children write **hot, nut**

a. You're going to write the word **hot**. Think about the sounds in (pause) **hot** and write the word. ✓
b. (Repeat *a* for **nut**.)

END OF SPELLING LESSON 46

Lesson 47

WORD WRITING

Children write **mad, mud, sad**

a. You're going to write the word **mad**. Listen. **Mad.** Saying the sounds in (pause) **mad** the hard way. Get ready. (Signal for each sound as the children say) *mmm* (pause) *aaa* (pause) *d.* (The children are to pause between the sounds. Repeat until firm.)
b. Everybody, write the word (pause) **mad**. ✓
c. (Repeat *a* and *b* for **mud, sad**.)

Children write **mat, on**

a. You're going to write the word **mat**. Think about the sounds in (pause) **mat** and write the word. ✓

To correct

1. Say the sounds in **mat.** (Signal.)
   Mmmaaat.
2. Say the sounds the hard way.
   (Signal.) *Mmm* (pause) *aaa*
   (pause) *t.*
3. Write the word **mat.** ✓

b. (Repeat *a* for **on.**)

Children write **had**

a. You're going to write the word (pause)
   had. This word rhymes with **sad.** I'll
   say the sounds in (pause) **had** the
   hard way. Listen. **H** (pause) **aaa**
   (pause) **d.**
b. Your turn. Say the sounds in (pause)
   had. Get ready. (Signal for each
   sound as the children say) *h* (pause)
   aaa (pause) *d.* (The children are to
   pause between the sounds. Repeat
   until firm.)
c. Everybody, write the word (pause)
   had. ✓

Children write **sit**

You're going to write the word **sit.**
Think about the sounds in (pause) **sit**
and write the word. ✓

END OF SPELLING LESSON 47

Lesson 48

WORD WRITING

Children write **hot, sad**

a. You're going to write the word **hot.**
   Think about the sounds in (pause) **hot**
   and write the word. ✓

To correct

1. Say the sounds in **hot.** (Signal.)
   Hooot.
2. Say the sounds the hard way.
   (Signal.) *H* (pause) *ooo* (pause) *t.*
3. Write the word **hot.** ✓

b. (Repeat *a* for **sad.**)

Children write **nod**

a. You're going to write the word **nod.**
   Listen. **Nod.** Saying the sounds in
   (pause) **nod** the hard way. Get ready.
   (Signal for each sound as the children
   say) *nnn* (pause) *ooo* (pause) *d.* (The
   children are to pause between the
   sounds. Repeat until firm.)
b. Everybody, write the word (pause)
   nod. ✓

Children write **hum, his, him, nut, has**

a. You're going to write the word **hum.**
   Think about the sounds in (pause)
   hum and write the word. ✓
b. You're going to write the word **his.**
   Think about the sounds in (pause) **his**
   and write the word. ✓

To correct

1. Say the sounds the hard way.
   (Signal.) *H* (pause) *iii* (pause) *sss.*
2. Write the word **his.** ✓

c. (Repeat *a* for **him, nut.**)
d. (Repeat *b* for **has.**)

END OF SPELLING LESSON 48

Lesson 49

WORD WRITING

Children write **sad, sun**

a. You're going to write the word **sad.**
   Think about the sounds in (pause)
   sad and write the word. ✓

To correct
1. Say the sounds in **sad.** (Signal.) *Sssaaad.*
2. Say the sounds the hard way. (Signal.) *Sss* (pause) *aaa* (pause) *d.*
3. Write the word **sad.** ✓

b. (Repeat *a* for **sun.**)

Children write **rid**

a. You're going to write the word **rid.** Listen. **Rid.** Saying the sounds in (pause) **rid** the hard way. Get ready. (Signal for each sound as the children say) *rrr* (pause) *iii* (pause) *d.* (The children are to pause between the sounds. Repeat until firm.)
b. Everybody, write the word (pause) **rid.** ✓

EXERCISE 3

Children write **run, mad, it, mud, sit**

a. You're going to write the word **run.** Think about the sounds in (pause) **run** and write the word. ✓
b. (Repeat *a* for **mad, it, mud, sit.**)

END OF SPELLING LESSON 49

Lesson 50

WORD WRITING

EXERCISE 1

Children write **an, ran**

a. You're going to write the word **an.** Think about the sounds in (pause) **an** and write the word. ✓

To correct
1. Say the sounds in **an.** (Signal.) *Aaannn.*
2. Say the sounds the hard way. (Signal.) *Aaa* (pause) *nnn.*
3. Write the word **an.** ✓

b. (Repeat *a* for **ran.**)

EXERCISE 2

Children write **dan, tan**

a. You're going to write the word (pause) **dan.** It rhymes with **ran.** This word is tough. I'll say the sounds in (pause) **dan** the hard way. Listen **D** (pause) **aaa** (pause) **nnn.**
b. Your turn. Say the sounds in (pause) **dan.** Get ready. (Signal for each sound as the children say) *d* (pause) *aaa* (pause) *nnn.* (The children are to pause between sounds. Repeat until firm.)
c. Everybody, write the word (pause) **dan.** ✓

---

d. Now you're going to write the word (pause) **Tan.** It rhymes with **ran.** This word is tough. I'll say the sounds in (pause) **tan** the hard way. Listen **T** (pause) **aaa** (pause) **nnn.**
e. Your turn. Say the sounds in (pause) **tan.** Get ready. (Signal for each sound as the children say) *t* (pause) *aaa* (pause) *nnn.* (The children are to pause between sounds. Repeat until firm.)
f. Everybody, write the word (pause) **tan.** ✓

EXERCISE 3

Children write **sun, fin, nut, mud, it, rat**

a. You're going to write the word **sun.** Think about the sounds in (pause) **sun** and write the word. ✓
b. (Repeat *a* for **fin, nut, mud, it, rat.**)

END OF SPELLING LESSON 50

Lesson 51

WORD WRITING

EXERCISE 1

Children write mud

You're going to write the word **mud.** Think about the sounds in (pause) **mud** and write the word. ✓

> **To correct**
> 1. Say the sounds in **mud.** (Signal.) *Mmmuuud.*
> 2. Say the sounds the hard way. (Signal.) *Mmm* (pause) *uuu* (pause) *d.*
> 3. Write the word **mud.** ✓

EXERCISE 2

Children write tan

a. You're going to write the word (pause) **tan.** This word rhymes with **ran.** I'll say the sounds in (pause) **tan** the hard way. Listen. **T** (pause) *aaa* (pause) **nnn.**
b. Your turn. Say the sounds in (pause) **tan.** Get ready. (Signal for each sound as the children say) *t* (pause) *aaa* (pause) *nnn.* (The children are to pause between sounds. Repeat until firm.)
c. Everybody, write the word (pause) **tan.** ✓

EXERCISE 3

Children write not, fin, hat, fat, his, him

a. You're going to write the word **not.** Think about the sounds in (pause) **not** and write the word. ✓
b. (Repeat *a* for **fin, hat, fat.**)
c. You're going to write the word **his.** Think about the sounds in (pause) **his** and write the word. ✓

> **To correct**
> 1. Say the sounds the hard way. (Signal.) *H* (pause) *iii* (pause) *sss.*
> 2. Write the word **his.** ✓

d. (Repeat *a* for **him.**)

END OF SPELLING LESSON 51

Lesson 52

WORD WRITING

EXERCISE 1

Children write ron, an

a. You're going to write the word **ron.** Think about the sounds in (pause) **ron** and write the word. ✓

> **To correct**
> 1. Say the sounds in **ron.** (Signal.) *Rrrooonnn.*
> 2. Say the sounds the hard way. (Signal.) *Rrr* (pause) *ooo* (pause) *nnn.*
> 3. Write the word **ron.** ✓

b. (Repeat *a* for **an.**)

EXERCISE 2

Children write and

a. You're going to write the word **and.** Listen. **And.** Saying the sounds in (pause) **and** the hard way. Get ready. (Signal for each sound as the children say) *aaa* (pause) *nnn* (pause) *d.* (The children are to pause between the sounds. Repeat until firm.)
b. Everybody, write the word (pause) **and.** ✓

EXERCISE 3

Children write hit

You're going to write the word **hit.** Think about the sounds in (pause) **hit** and write the word. ✓

EXERCISE 4

Children write **tan**

a. You're going to write the word (pause) **tan.** This word rhymes with **ran.** I'll say the sounds in (pause) **tan** the hard way. Listen. **T** (pause) **aaa** (pause) **nnn.**

b. Your turn. Say the sounds in (pause) **tan.** Get ready. (Signal for each sound as the children say) *t* (pause) *aaa* (pause) *nnn.* (The children are to pause between the sounds. Repeat until firm.)

c. Everybody, write the word (pause) **tan.** ✓

EXERCISE 5

Children write **sit, his**

a. You're going to write the word **sit.** Think about the sounds in (pause) **sit** and write the word. ✓

b. (Repeat *a* for **his.**)

END OF SPELLING LESSON 52

Lesson 53

WORD WRITING

EXERCISE 1

Children write **me**

a. You're going to write the word **me.** Listen. **Me.** Saying the sounds in (pause) **me** the hard way. Get ready. (Signal for each sound as the children say) *mmm* (pause) *ēēē.* (The children are to pause between the sounds. Repeat until firm.)

b. Everybody, write the word (pause) **me.** ✓

EXERCISE 2

Children write **he**

a. You're going to write the word (pause) **he.** It rhymes with **me.** This word is tough. I'll say the sounds in (pause) **he** the hard way. Listen. **H** (pause one second) **ēēē.**

b. Your turn. Say the sounds in (pause) **he.** Get ready. (Signal for each sound as the children say) *h* (pause) *ēēē.* (The children are to pause between the sounds. Repeat until firm.)

c. Everybody, write the word (pause) **he.** ✓

EXERCISE 3

Children write **ham**

a. You're going to write the word **ham.** Think about the sounds in (pause) **ham** and write the word. ✓

EXERCISE 4

Children write **and**

a. You're going to write the word **and.** Listen. **And.** Saying the sounds in (pause) **and** the hard way. Get ready. (Signal for each sound as the children say) *aaa* (pause) *nnn* (pause) *d.* (The children are to pause between the sounds. Repeat until firm.)

b. Everybody, write the word (pause) **and.** ✓

EXERCISE 5

Children write **hand**

a. You're going to write the word (pause) **hand.** It rhymes with **and.** This word is tough. I'll say the sounds in (pause) **hand** the hard way. Listen. **H** (pause) **aaa** (pause) **nnn** (pause) **d.**

b. Your turn. Say the sounds in (pause) **hand.** Get ready. (Signal for each sound as the children say) *h* (pause) *aaa* (pause) *nnn* (pause) *d.* (The children are to pause between sounds. Repeat until firm.)

c. Everybody, write the word (pause) **hand.** ✓

EXERCISE 6

Children write **mud, fit**

a. You're going to write the word **mud.** Think about the sounds in (pause) **mud** and write the word. ✓

b. (Repeat *a* for **fit.**)

END OF SPELLING LESSON 53

Lesson 54

WORD WRITING

EXERCISE 1

Children write **me, he**

a. You're going to write the word **me.** Listen. **Me.** Saying the sounds in (pause) **me** the hard way. Get ready. (Signal for each sound as the children say) *mmm* (pause) *ēēē.* (The children are to pause between the sounds. Repeat until firm.)

b. Everybody, write the word (pause) **me.** ✓

c. (Repeat *a* and *b* for **he.**)

EXERCISE 2

Children write **tan, fit, mad, rid, sad, mud**

a. You're going to write the word **tan.** Think about the sounds in (pause) **tan** and write the word. ✓

> **To correct**
> 1. Say the sounds in **tan.** (Signal.) *Taaannn.*
> 2. Say the sounds the hard way. (Signal.) *T* (pause) *aaa* (pause) *nnn.*
> 3. Write the word **tan.** ✓

b. (Repeat *a* for **fit, mad, rid, sad, mud.**)

EXERCISE 3

Children write **and**

a. You're going to write the word **and.** Listen. **And.** Saying the sounds in (pause) **and** the hard way. Get ready. (Signal for each sound as the children say) *aaa* (pause) *nnn* (pause) *d.* (The children are to pause between the sounds. Repeat until firm.)

b. Everybody, write the word (pause) **and.** ✓

EXERCISE 4

Children write **hand**

a. You're going to write the word (pause) **hand.** This word rhymes with **and.** I'll say the sounds in (pause) **hand** the hard way. Listen. **H** (pause) **aaa** (pause) **nnn** (pause) **d.**

b. Your turn. Say the sounds in (pause) **hand.** Get ready. (Signal for each sound as the children say) *h* (pause) *aaa* (pause) *nnn* (pause) *d.* (The children are to pause between the sounds. Repeat until firm.)

c. Everybody, write the word (pause) **hand.** ✓

EXERCISE 5

Children write **fan, sin**

a. You're going to write the word **fan.** Think about the sounds in (pause) **fan** and write the word. ✓

b. (Repeat *a* for **sin.**)

END OF SPELLING LESSON 54

Lesson 55

WORD WRITING

EXERCISE 1

Children write he

a. You're going to write the word **he**. Listen. **He.** Saying the sounds in (pause) **he** the hard way. Get ready. (Signal for each sound as the children say) *h* (pause) *ēēē*. (The children are to pause between the sounds. Repeat until firm.)

b. Everybody, write the word (pause) **he.** ✓

EXERCISE 2

Children write hand

a. You're going to write the word (pause) **hand.** This word is tough. I'll say the sounds in (pause) **hand** the hard way. Listen. **H** (pause) **aaa** (pause) **nnn** (pause) **d.**

b. Your turn. Say the sounds in (pause) **hand.** Get ready. (Signal for each sound as the children say) *h* (pause) *aaa* (pause) *nnn* (pause) *d.* (The children are to pause between the sounds. Repeat until firm.)

c. Everybody, write the word (pause) **hand.** ✓

EXERCISE 3

Children write tan, dan, in

a. You're going to write the word **tan.** Think about the sounds in (pause) **tan** and write the word. ✓

> **To correct**
> 1. Say the sounds in **tan.** (Signal.) *Taaannn.*
> 2. Say the sounds the hard way. (Signal.) *T* (pause) *aaa* (pause) *nnn.*
> 3. Write the word **tan.** ✓

b. (Repeat *a* for **dan, in.**)

EXERCISE 4

Children write tin

a. You're going to write the word (pause) **tin.** This word rhymes with **in.** I'll say the sounds in (pause) **tin** the hard way. Listen. **T** (pause) **iii** (pause) **nnn.**

b. Your turn. Say the sounds in (pause) **tin.** Get ready. (Signal for each sound as the children say) *t* (pause) *iii* (pause) *nnn.* (The children are to pause between the sounds. Repeat until firm.)

c. Everybody, write the word (pause) **tin.** ✓

END OF SPELLING LESSON 55

Lesson 56

WORD WRITING

EXERCISE 1

Children write we, had

a. You're going to write the word **we.** Listen. **We.** Saying the sounds in (pause) **we** the hard way. Get ready. (Signal for each sound as the children say) *www* (pause) *ēēē*. (The children are to pause between the sounds. Repeat until firm.)

b. Everybody, write the word (pause) **we.** ✓

c. (Repeat *a* and *b* for **had.**)

EXERCISE 2

Children write fit, if, on, he, sin, fan, has

a. You're going to write the word **fit.** Think about the sounds in (pause) **fit** and write the word. ✓

b. (Repeat *a* for **if, on, he, sin, fan, has.**)

END OF SPELLING LESSON 56

Lesson 57

WORD WRITING

EXERCISE 1

Children write dan, on, hand, has, not, run

a. You're going to write the word **dan.** Think about the sounds in (pause) **dan** and write the word. ✓

> **To correct**
> 1. Say the sounds in **dan.** (Signal.) *Daaannn.*
> 2. Say the sounds the hard way. (Signal.) *D* (pause) *aaa* (pause) *nnn.*
> 3. Write the word **dan.** ✓

b. (Repeat *a* for **on, hand, has, not, run.**)

EXERCISE 2

Children write we, win

a. You're going to write the word **we.** Listen. **We.** Saying the sounds in (pause) **we** the hard way. Get ready. (Signal for each sound as the children say) *www* (pause) *ēēē.* (The children are to pause between the sounds. Repeat until firm.)

b. Everybody, write the word (pause) **we.** ✓

c. (Repeat *a* and *b* for **win.**)

EXERCISE 3

Children write in, sun, he, it, at

a. You're going to write the word **in.** Think about the sounds in (pause) **in** and write the word. ✓

b. (Repeat *a* for **sun, he, it, at.**)

END OF SPELLING LESSON 57

Lesson 58

WORD WRITING

EXERCISE 1

Children write we, an, at, if, is, and, has, his

a. You're going to write the word **we.** Think about the sounds in (pause) **we** and write the word. ✓

> **To correct**
> 1. Say the sounds in **we.** (Signal.) *Wwwēēē.*
> 2. Say the sounds the hard way. (Signal.) *Www* (pause) *ēēē.*
> 3. Write the word **we.** ✓

b. (Repeat *a* for **an, at, if.**)

c. You're going to write the word **is.** Think about the sounds in (pause) **is** and write the word. ✓

> **To correct**
> 1. Say the sounds the hard way. (Signal.) *iii* (pause) *sss.*
> 2. Write the word **is.** ✓

d. (Repeat *a* for **and.**)

e. (Repeat *c* for **has, his.**)

END OF SPELLING LESSON 58

Lesson 59

WORD WRITING

EXERCISE 1

Children write he, tan, mad, we, win, and, nut

a. You're going to write the word **he.** Think about the sounds in (pause) **he** and write the word. ✓

> **To correct**
> 1. Say the sounds in **he.** (Signal.) *Hēēē.*
> 2. Say the sounds the hard way. (Signal.) *H* (pause) *ēēē.*
> 3. Write the word **he.** ✓

b. (Repeat *a* for **tan, mad, we, win, and, nut.**)

EXERCISE 2

Children write **land**

a. You're going to write the word **land**. Listen. **Land.** Saying the sounds in (pause) **land** the hard way. Get ready. (Signal for each sound as the children say) *lll* (pause) *aaa* (pause) *nnn* (pause) *d.* (The children are to pause between the sounds. Repeat until firm.)

b. Everybody, write the word (pause) **land.** ✓

EXERCISE 3

Children write **has, mud, hand, rid**

a. You're going to write the word **has.** Think about the sounds in (pause) **has** and write the word. ✓

> **To correct**
> 1. Say the sounds the hard way. (Signal.) *H* (pause) *aaa* (pause) *sss.*
> 2. Write the word **has.** ✓

b. (Repeat *a* for **mud, hand, rid.**)

END OF SPELLING LESSON 59

Lesson 60

WORD WRITING

EXERCISE 1

Children write **nod**

a. You're going to write the word **nod.** Listen. **Nod.** Saying the sounds in (pause) **nod** the hard way. Get ready. (Signal for each sound as the children say) *nnn* (pause) *ooo* (pause) *d.* (The children are to pause between the sounds. Repeat until firm.)

b. Everybody, write the word (pause) **nod.** ✓

EXERCISE 2

Children write **and, hand, land**

a. You're going to write the word **and.** Think about the sounds in (pause) **and** and write the word. ✓

> **To correct**
> 1. Say the sounds in **and.** (Signal.) *Aaannnd.*
> 2. Say the sounds the hard way. (Signal.) *Aaa* (pause) *nnn* (pause) *d.*
> 3. Write the word **and.** ✓

b. (Repeat *a* for **hand, land.**)

EXERCISE 3

Children write **rid, lid**

a. You're going to write the word **rid.** Listen. **Rid.** Saying the sounds in (pause) **rid** the hard way. Get ready. (Signal for each sound as the children say) *rrr* (pause) *iii* (pause) *d.* (The children are to pause between the sounds. Repeat until firm.)

b. Everybody, write the word (pause) **rid.** ✓

c. (Repeat *a* and *b* for **lid**.)

EXERCISE 4

Children write **if, has, tin, we**

a. You're going to write the word **if.** Think about the sounds in (pause) **if** and write the word. ✓

b. (Repeat *a* for **has, tin, we.**)

END OF SPELLING LESSON 60

Lesson 61

WORD WRITING

EXERCISE 1

Children write hand, we, land, me, has

a. You're going to write the word **hand**. Think about the sounds in (pause) **hand** and write the word. ✓

b. (Repeat *a* for **we, land, me**.)

c. You're going to write the word **has**. Think about the sounds in (pause) **has** and write the word. ✓

> **To correct**
> 1. Say the sounds the hard way. (Signal.) *H* (pause) *aaa* (pause) *sss*.
> 2. Write the word **has**. ✓

EXERCISE 2

Children write win, nod

a. You're going to write the word **win**. Listen. **Win.** Saying the sounds in (pause) **win** the hard way. Get ready. (Signal for each sound as the children say) *www* (pause) *iii* (pause) *nnn*. (The children are to pause between the sounds. Repeat until firm.)

b. Everybody, write the word (pause) **win**. ✓

c. (Repeat *a* and *b* for **nod**.)

EXERCISE 3

Children write sit, lit, fit

a. You're going to write the word **sit**. Think about the sounds in (pause) **sit** and write the word. ✓

b. (Repeat *a* for **lit, fit**.)

END OF SPELLING LESSON 61

Lesson 62

WORD WRITING

EXERCISE 1

Children write hot, hand, mud, tan, dan, nut, if, land

a. You're going to write the word **hot**. Think about the sounds in (pause) **hot** and write the word. ✓

> **To correct**
> 1. Say the sounds in **hot**. (Signal.) *Hooot*.
> 2. Say the sounds the hard way. (Signal.) *H* (pause) *ooo* (pause) *t*.
> 3. Write the word **hot**. ✓

b. (Repeat *a* for **hand, mud, tan, dan, nut, if, land**.)

END OF SPELLING LESSON 62

Lesson 63

WORD WRITING

EXERCISE 1

Children write nod, fit, tan, dan, fin, tin, his

a. You're going to write the word **nod**. Think about the sounds in (pause) **nod** and write the word. ✓

> **To correct**
> 1. Say the sounds in **nod**. (Signal.) *Nnnoood*.
> 2. Say the sounds the hard way. (Signal.) *Nnn* (pause) *ooo* (pause) *d*.
> 3. Write the word **nod**. ✓

b. (Repeat *a* for **fit, tan, dan, fin, tin**.)

c. You're going to write the word **his**. Think about the sounds in (pause) **his** and write the word. ✓

> **To correct**
> 1. Say the sounds the hard way. (Signal.) *H* (pause) *iii* (pause) *sss*.
> 2. Write the word **his**. ✓

END OF SPELLING LESSON 63

Lesson 64

WORD WRITING

EXERCISE 1

Children write did, rid, hid

a. You're going to write the word **did.** Listen. **Did.** Saying the sounds in (pause) **did** the hard way. Get ready. (Signal for each sound as the children say) *d* (pause) *iii* (pause) *d.* (The children are to pause between the sounds. Repeat until firm.)

b. Everybody, write the word (pause) **did.** ✓

c. (Repeat *a* and *b* for **rid, hid.**)

EXERCISE 2

Children write sin, tin, hand

a. You're going to write the word **sin.** Think about the sounds in (pause) **sin** and write the word. ✓

> **To correct**
> 1. Say the sounds in **sin.** (Signal.) *Sssiiinnn.*
> 2. Say the sounds the hard way. (Signal.) *Sss* (pause) *iii* (pause) *nnn.*
> 3. Write the word **sin.** ✓

b. (Repeat *a* for **tin, hand.**)

EXERCISE 3

Children write sand

a. You're going to write the word **sand.** Listen. **Sand.** Saying the sounds in (pause) **sand** the hard way. Get ready. (Signal for each sound as the children say) *sss* (pause) *aaa* (pause) *nnn* (pause) *d.* (The children are to pause between the sounds. Repeat until firm.)

b. Everybody, write the word (pause) **sand.** ✓

END OF SPELLING LESSON 64

Lesson 65

WORD WRITING

EXERCISE 1

Children write did, dad

a. You're going to write the word **did.** Listen. **Did.** Saying the sounds in (pause) **did** the hard way. Get ready. (Signal for each sound as the children say) *d* (pause) *iii* (pause) *d.* (The children are to pause between the sounds. Repeat until firm.)

b. Everybody, write the word (pause) **did.** ✓

c. (Repeat *a* and *b* for **dad.**)

EXERCISE 2

Children write sand

a. You're going to write the word **sand.** Listen. **Sand.** Saying the sounds in (pause) **sand** the hard way. Get ready. (Signal for each sound as the children say) *sss* (pause) *aaa* (pause) *nnn* (pause) *d.* (The children are to pause between the sounds. Repeat until firm.)

b. Everybody, write the word (pause) **sand.** ✓

EXERCISE 3

Children write not, me, his, tin

a. You're going to write the word **not.** Think about the sounds in (pause) **not** and write the word. ✓

> **To correct**
> 1. Say the sounds in **not.** (Signal.) *Nnnooot.*
> 2. Say the sounds the hard way. (Signal.) *Nnn* (pause) *ooo* (pause) *t.*
> 3. Write the word **not.** ✓

b. (Repeat *a* for **me.**)

c. You're going to write the word **his.** Think about the sounds in (pause) **his** and write the word. ✓

To correct
1. Say the sounds the hard way. (Signal.) *H* (pause) *iii* (pause) *sss.*
2. Write the word **his.** ✓

d. (Repeat *c* for **tin.**)

END OF SPELLING LESSON 65

Lesson 66

WORD WRITING

EXERCISE 1

Children write **sun, sit, he, sad**

a. You're going to write the word **sun.** Think about the sounds in (pause) **sun** and write the word. ✓

To correct
1. Say the sounds in **sun.** (Signal.) *Sssuuunnn.*
2. Say the sounds the hard way. (Signal.) *Sss* (pause) *uuu* (pause) *nnn.*
3. Write the word **sun.** ✓

b. (Repeat *a* for **sit, he, sad.**)

EXERCISE 2

Children write **dad**

a. You're going to write the word **dad.** Listen. **Dad.** Saying the sounds in (pause) **dad** the hard way. Get ready. (Signal for each sound as the children say) *d* (pause) *aaa* (pause) *d.* (The children are to pause between the sounds. Repeat until firm.)
b. Everybody, write the word (pause) **dad.** ✓

EXERCISE 3

Children write **had, ron, fit**

a. You're going to write the word **had.** Think about the sounds in (pause) **had** and write the word. ✓
b. (Repeat *a* for **ron, fit.**)

END OF SPELLING LESSON 66

Lesson 67

WORD WRITING

EXERCISE 1

Children write **did, hid**

a. You're going to write the word **did.** Listen. **Did.** Saying the sounds in (pause) **did** the hard way. Get ready. (Signal for each sound as the children say) *d* (pause) *iii* (pause) *d.* (The children are to pause between the sounds. Repeat until firm.)
b. Everybody, write the word (pause) **did.** ✓
c. (Repeat *a* and *b* for **hid.**)

EXERCISE 2

Children write **land, not**

a. You're going to write the word **land.** Think about the sounds in (pause) **land** and write the word. ✓

To correct
1. Say the sounds in **land.** (Signal.) *Lllaaannnd.*
2. Say the sounds the hard way. (Signal.) *Lll* (pause) *aaa* (pause) *nnn* (pause) *d.*
3. Write the word **land.** ✓

b. (Repeat *a* for **not.**)

Children write **has, mud, hot, we, win**

a. You're going to write the word **has.** Think about the sounds in (pause) **has** and write the word. ✓

> **To correct**
> 1. Say the sounds the hard way. (Signal.) *H* (pause) *aaa* (pause) *sss.*
> 2. Write the word **has.** ✓

b. You're going to write the word **mud.** Think about the sounds in (pause) **mud** and write the word. ✓

> **To correct**
> 1. Say the sounds in **mud.** (Signal.) *Mmmuuud.*
> 2. Say the sounds the hard way. (Signal.) *Mmm* (pause) *uuu* (pause) *d.*
> 3. Write the word **mud.** ✓

c. (Repeat *b* for **hot, we, win.**)

END OF SPELLING LESSON 67

Lesson 68

WORD WRITING

Children write **and, land, sand, hand, if, has, is, on, tin, win**

a. You're going to write the word **and.** Think about the sounds in (pause) **and** and write the word. ✓

> **To correct**
> 1. Say the sounds in **and.** (Signal.) *Aaannnd.*
> 2. Say the sounds the hard way. (Signal.) *Aaa* (pause) *nnn* (pause) *d.*
> 3. Write the word **and.** ✓

b. (Repeat *a* for **land, sand, hand, if.**)

c. You're going to write the word **has.** Think about the sounds in (pause) **has** and write the word. ✓

> **To correct**
> 1. Say the sounds the hard way. (Signal.) *H* (pause) *aaa* (pause) *sss.*
> 2. Write the word **has.** ✓

d. (Repeat *c* for **is, on, tin, win.**)

END OF SPELLING LESSON 68

Lesson 69

WORD WRITING

Children write **win**

a. You're going to write the word **win.** Listen. **Win.** Saying the sounds in (pause) **win** the hard way. Get ready. (Signal for each sound as the children say) *www* (pause) *iii* (pause) *nnn.* (The children are to pause between the sounds. Repeat until firm.)

b. Everybody, write the word (pause) **win.** ✓

Children write **and**

You're going to write the word **and.** Think about the sounds in (pause) **and** and write the word. ✓

Children write **ant**

a. You're going to write the word (pause) **ant.** Say the sounds you write for (pause) **ant.** Get ready. (Signal for each sound as the children say) *aaa* (pause) *nnn* (pause) *t.* (The children are to pause between the sounds. Repeat until firm.)

b. Everybody, write the word (pause) **ant.** ✓

Children write **we, sit, he, fat, me**

a. You're going to write the word **we.** Think about the sounds in (pause) **we** and write the word. ✓

b. (Repeat *a* for **sit, he, fat, me.**)

END OF SPELLING LESSON 69

Lesson 70

WORD WRITING

Children write **me, has, lid**

a. You're going to write the word **me.** Think about the sounds in (pause) **me** and write the word. ✓

> **To correct**
> 1. Say the sounds in **me.** (Signal.) *Mmmēēē.*
> 2. Say the sounds the hard way. (Signal.) *Mmm* (pause) *ēēē.*
> 3. Write the word **me.** ✓

b. Now you're going to write the word **has.** Think about the sounds in (pause) **has** and write the word. ✓

> **To correct**
> 1. Say the sounds the hard way. (Signal.) *H* (pause) *aaa* (pause) *sss.*
> 2. Write the word **has.** ✓

c. (Repeat *b* for **lid.**)

Children write **was**

a. You're going to write the word **was.** When you write the word (pause) **was,** you write these sounds. **Www** (pause) **aaa** (pause) **sss.**

b. Say the sounds you write for (pause) **was.** (Signal for each sound as the children say) *www* (pause) *aaa* (pause) *sss.* (The children are to pause between the sounds. Repeat until firm.)

c. Everybody, write the word (pause) **was.** ✓

Children write **dad**

a. You're going to write the word **dad.** Listen. **Dad.** Saying the sounds in (pause) **dad** the hard way. Get ready. (Signal for each sound as the children say) *d* (pause) *aaa* (pause) *d.* (The children are to pause between the sounds. Repeat until firm.)

b. Everybody, write the word (pause) **dad.** ✓

Children write **tin, an, ant, we**

a. You're going to write the word **tin.** Think about the sounds in (pause) **tin** and write the word. ✓

> **To correct**
> 1. Say the sounds in **tin.** (Signal.) *Tiiinnn.*
> 2. Say the sounds the hard way. (Signal.) *T* (pause) *iii* (pause) *nnn.*
> 3. Write the word **tin.** ✓

b. (Repeat *a* for **an, ant, we.**)

END OF SPELLING LESSON 70

Lesson 71

WORD WRITING

Children write **we, has**

a. You're going to write the word **we.** Think about the sounds in (pause) **we** and write the word. ✓

> **To correct**
> 1. Say the sounds in **we.** (Signal.) *Wwwēēē.*
> 2. Say the sounds the hard way. (Signal.) *Www* (pause) *ēēē.*
> 3. Write the word **we.** ✓

b. Now you're going to write the word
has. Think about the sounds in
(pause) **has** and write the word. ✓

> **To correct**
> 1. Say the sounds the hard way.
>   (Signal.) *H* (pause) *aaa* (pause) *sss.*
> 2. Write the word **has.** ✓

EXERCISE 2

Children write **was**

a. You're going to write the word (pause)
was. When you write the word (pause)
was, you write these sounds. **Www**
(pause) **aaa** (pause) **sss.**

b. Say the sounds you write for (pause)
was. (Signal for each sound as the
children say) *www* (pause) *aaa*
(pause) *sss.* (The children are to
pause between sounds. Repeat until
firm.)

c. Everybody, write the word (pause)
was. ✓

EXERCISE 3

Children write **tin, land, sand, hid, lid**

a. You're going to write the word **tin.**
Think about the sounds in (pause) **tin**
and write the word. ✓

b. (Repeat *a* for **land, sand, hid, lid.**)

END OF SPELLING LESSON 71

Lesson 72

WORD WRITING

EXERCISE 1

Children write **has**

You're going to write the word **has.**
Think about the sounds in (pause)
has and write the word. ✓

> **To correct**
> 1. Say the sounds the hard way.
>   (Signal.) *H* (pause) *aaa* (pause) *sss.*
> 2. Write the word **has.** ✓

EXERCISE 2

Children write **was**

a. You're going to write the word (pause)
was. When you write the word (pause)
was, you write these sounds. **Www**
(pause) **aaa** (pause) **sss.**

b. Say the sounds you write for (pause)
was. (Signal for each sound as the
children say) *www* (pause) *aaa*
(pause) *sss.* (The children are to
pause between sounds. Repeat until
firm.)

c. Everybody, write the word (pause)
was. ✓

EXERCISE 3

Children write **hid, did, dad, tin, mud**

a. You're going to write the word **hid.**
Think about the sounds in (pause) **hid**
and write the word. ✓

> **To correct**
> 1. Say the sounds in **hid.** *Hiiid.*
> 2. Say the sounds the hard way. *H*
>   (pause) *iii* (pause) *d.*
> 3. Write the word **hid.** ✓

b. (Repeat *a* for **did, dad, tin, mud.**)

END OF SPELLING LESSON 72

Lesson 73

WORD WRITING

EXERCISE 1

Children write **is, has, his**

a. You're going to write the word **is.**
Think about the sounds in (pause) **is**
and write the word. ✓

> **To correct**
> 1. Say the sounds the hard way.
>   (Signal.) *iii* (pause) *sss.*
> 2. Write the word **is.** ✓

b. (Repeat *a* for **has, his.**)

Children write **was**

a. You're going to write the word (pause) **was.** Say the sounds you write for (pause) **was.** Get ready. (Signal for each sound as the children say) *www* (pause) *aaa* (pause) *sss.* (The children are to pause between the sounds. Repeat until firm.)

b. Everybody, write the word (pause) **was.** ✓

SENTENCE WRITING

Children write a sentence

Children are not responsible for capital letters.

a. Listen to this sentence. **He hit me.** Your turn. Say that sentence. Get ready. (Signal.) *He hit me.*

b. Now you're going to say it the slow way. Get ready. (Signal for each word as the children say) *He* (pause) *hit* (pause) *me.* (Repeat until firm.)

c. Everybody, write the sentence. Spell each word the right way. (As you check children's responses, remind the children:) Don't forget to put a period at the end of your sentence.

END OF SPELLING LESSON 73

Lesson 74

WORD WRITING

Children write **was**

a. You're going to write the word (pause) **was.** Say the sounds you write for (pause) **was.** Get ready. (Signal for each sound as the children say) *www* (pause) *aaa* (pause) *sss.* (The children are to pause between the sounds. Repeat until firm.)

b. Everybody, write the word (pause) **was.** ✓

Children write **tin, did, we, mad, win**

a. You're going to write the word **tin.** Think about the sounds in (pause) **tin** and write the word. ✓

> **To correct**
> 1. Say the sounds in **tin.** (Signal.) *Tiiinnn.*
> 2. Say the sounds the hard way. (Signal.) *T* (pause) *iii* (pause) *nnn.*
> 3. Write the word **tin.** ✓

b. (Repeat *a* for **did, we, mad, win.**)

SENTENCE WRITING

Children write a sentence

a. Listen to this sentence. **We had sand.** Your turn. Say that sentence. Get ready. (Signal.) *We had sand.*

b. Now you're going to say it the slow way. Get ready. (Signal for each word as the children say) *We* (pause) *had* (pause) *sand.* (Repeat until firm.)

c. Everybody, write the sentence. Spell each word the right way. (As you check children's responses, remind the children:) Don't forget to put a period at the end of your sentence.

END OF SPELLING LESSON 74

Lesson 75

WORD WRITING

Children write **can**

a. You're going to write the word (pause) **can.** This word rhymes with **man.** I'll say the sounds in (pause) **can** the hard way. Listen. **C** (pause) **aaa** (pause) **nnn.**

b. Your turn. Say the sounds in (pause) **can.** Get ready. (Signal for each sound as the children say) *c* (pause) *aaa* (pause) *nnn.* (The children are to pause between sounds. Repeat until firm.)

c. Everybody, write the word (pause) **can.** ✓

EXERCISE 2

Children write **has**

You're going to write the word **has.** Think about the sounds in (pause) **has** and write the word. ✓

> **To correct**
> 1. Say the sounds the hard way. (Signal.) *H* (pause) *aaa* (pause) *sss.*
> 2. Write the word **has.** ✓

EXERCISE 3

Children write **was**

a. You're going to write the word (pause) **was.** Say the sounds you write for (pause) **was.** Get ready. (Signal for each sound as the children say) *www* (pause) *aaa* (pause) *sss.* (The children are to pause between the sounds. Repeat until firm.)

b. Everybody, write the word (pause) **was.** ✓

EXERCISE 4

Children write **land, nut**

a. You're going to write the word **land.** Think about the sounds in (pause) **land** and write the word. ✓

> **To correct**
> 1. Say the sounds in **land.** (Signal.) *Lllaaannnd.*
> 2. Say the sounds the hard way. (Signal.) *Lll* (pause) *aaa* (pause) *nnn* (pause) *d.*
> 3. Write the word **land.** ✓

b. (Repeat *a* for **nut.**)

SENTENCE WRITING

EXERCISE 5

Children write a sentence

a. Listen to this sentence. **He had fun.** Your turn. Say that sentence. Get ready. (Signal.) *He had fun.*

b. Now you're going to say it the slow way. Get ready. (Signal for each word as the children say) *he* (pause) *had* (pause) *fun.* (Repeat until firm.)

c. Everybody, write the sentence. Spell each word the right way. (As you check children's responses, remind the children:) Don't forget to put a period at the end of your sentence.

END OF SPELLING LESSON 75

Lesson 76

WORD WRITING

EXERCISE 1

Children write **can**

a. You're going to write the word (pause) **can.** This word rhymes with **man.** I'll say the sounds in (pause) **can** the hard way. Listen. **C** (pause) **aaa** (pause) **nnn.**

b. Your turn. Say the sounds in (pause) **can.** Get ready. (Signal for each sound as the children say) *c* (pause) *aaa* (pause) *nnn.* (The children are to pause between the sounds. Repeat until firm.)

c. Everybody, write the word (pause) **can.** ✓

EXERCISE 2

Children write **sand, fit, mud, tin**

a. You're going to write the word **sand.** Think about the sounds in (pause) **sand** and write the word. ✓

> **To correct**
> 1. Say the sounds in **sand.** (Signal.) *Sssaaannnd.*
> 2. Say the sounds the hard way. (Signal.) *Sss* (pause) *aaa* (pause) *nnn* (pause) *d.*
> 3. Write the word **sand.** ✓

b. (Repeat *a* for **fit, mud, tin.**)

SENTENCE WRITING

Children write a sentence

a. Listen to this sentence. **He was mad.** Your turn. Say that sentence. Get ready. (Signal.) *He was mad.*

b. Now you're going to say it the slow way. Get ready. (Signal for each word as the children say) *He* (pause) *was* (pause) *mad.* (Repeat until firm.)

c. Everybody, write the sentence. Spell each word the right way. (As you check children's responses, remind the children:) Don't forget to put a period at the end of your sentence.

END OF SPELLING LESSON 76

Lesson 77

WORD WRITING

EXERCISE 1

Children write if, am, hid, did

a. You're going to write the word **if.** Think about the sounds in (pause) **if** and write the word. ✓

To correct

1. Say the sounds in **if.** (Signal.) *iiifff.*
2. Say the sounds the hard way. (Signal.) *iii* (pause) *fff.*
3. Write the word **if.** ✓

---

b. (Repeat *a* for **am, hid, did.**)

SOUND WRITING

EXERCISE 2

Introduce sound combination ar

a. (Write on the board: **ar.**)
b. (Point to **ar.**) Everybody, these letters make the sound **are.** What sound? (Signal.) *Are. Yes,* **are.**
c. (Erase **ar.**) Everybody, write the two letters that go together and make the sound **are.** ✓

WORD WRITING

EXERCISE 3

Write sound combination words far, arm

a. (Write on the board: **far, arm.**)
b. (Point to **far.**) Everybody, read this word the fast way. Get ready. (Signal.) *Far. Yes,* **far.**
c. Everybody, say the sounds you write for the word (pause) **far.** Get ready. (Touch **f, ar** as the children say) *fff* (pause) *ar.* (Repeat until firm.)
d. (Erase **far.**) Everybody, write the word (pause) **far.** ✓
e. (Repeat *b* through *d* for **arm.**)

EXERCISE 4

Children write can

a. You're going to write the word (pause) **can.** This word rhymes with **man.** I'll say the sounds in (pause) **can** the hard way. Listen. **C** (pause) **aaa** (pause) **nnn.**

b. Your turn. Say the sounds in (pause) **can.** Get ready. (Signal for each sound as the children say) *c* (pause) *aaa* (pause) *nnn.* (The children are to pause between the sounds. Repeat until firm.)

c. Everybody, write the word (pause) **can.** ✓

SENTENCE WRITING

EXERCISE 5

Children write a sentence

a. Listen to this sentence. **He was fat.** Say the sentence. Get ready. (Signal.) *He was fat.*

b. Now you're going to say it the slow way. Get ready. (Signal for each word as the children say) *He* (pause) *was* (pause) *fat.* (Repeat until firm.)

c. Everybody, write the sentence. Spell each word the right way. (As you check children's responses, remind the children:) Don't forget to put a period at the end of your sentence.

END OF SPELLING LESSON 77

Lesson 78

WORD WRITING

EXERCISE 1

Children write ant, sun, can

a. You're going to write the word **ant**. Think about the sounds in (pause) **ant** and write the word. ✓

> **To correct**
> 1. Say the sounds in **ant**. (Signal.) *Aaannnt.*
> 2. Say the sounds the hard way. (Signal.) *Aaa* (pause) *nnn* (pause) *t.*
> 3. Write the word **ant**. ✓

b. (Repeat *a* for **sun, can**.)

SOUND WRITING

EXERCISE 2

Reinforce sound combination ar

a. (Write on the board: **ar**.)
b. (Point to **ar**.) Everybody, these letters make the sound **are**. What sound? (Signal.) *Are.* Yes, **are**.
c. (Erase **ar**.) Everybody, write the two letters that go together and make the sound **are**. ✓

WORD WRITING

EXERCISE 3

Write sound combination words far, arm, tar, car

a. (Write on the board: **far, arm, tar, car**.)
b. (Point to **far**.) Everybody, read this word the fast way. Get ready. (Signal.) *Far.* Yes, **far**.
c. Everybody, say the sounds you write for the word (pause) **far**. Get ready. (Touch **f, ar** as the children say) *fff* (pause) *ar.* (Repeat until firm.)
d. (Erase **far**.) Everybody, write the word (pause) **far**. ✓
e. (Repeat *b* through *d* for **arm, tar, car**.)

EXERCISE 4

Children write hot

You're going to write the word **hot**. Think about the sounds in (pause) **hot** and write the word. ✓

SENTENCE WRITING

EXERCISE 5

Children write a sentence

a. Listen to this sentence. **It is a nut.** Your turn. Say the sentence. Get ready. (Signal.) *It is a nut.*
b. Now you're going to say it the slow way. Get ready. (Signal for each word as the children say) *It* (pause) *is* (pause) *a* (pause) *nut.* (Repeat until firm.)
c. Everybody, write the sentence. Spell each word the right way. (As you check children's responses, remind the children:) Don't forget to put a period at the end of your sentence.

END OF SPELLING LESSON 78

Lesson 79

WORD WRITING

EXERCISE 1

Write sound combination words arm, farm

a. (Write on the board: **arm, farm**.)
b. (Point to **arm**.) Everybody, read this word the fast way. Get ready. (Signal.) *Arm.* Yes, **arm**.
c. Everybody, say the sounds you write for the word (pause) **arm**. Get ready. (Touch **ar, m** as the children say) *ar* (pause) *mmm.* (Repeat until firm.)
d. (Erase **arm**.) Everybody, write the word (pause) **arm**. ✓
e. (Repeat *b* through *d* for **farm**.)

Children write **not, and**

a. You're going to write the word **not.** Think about the sounds in (pause) **not** and write the word. ✓

> **To correct**
> 1. Say the sounds in **not.** (Signal.) *Nnnooot.*
> 2. Say the sounds the hard way. (Signal.) *Nnn* (pause) *ooo* (pause) *t.*
> 3. Write the word **not.** ✓

b. (Repeat *a* for **and.**)

EXERCISE 3

Children write **hid**

You're going to write the word **hid.** Think about the sounds in (pause) **hid** and write the word. ✓

SENTENCE WRITING

EXERCISE 4

Children write a sentence

a. Listen to this sentence. **It is hot.** Your turn. Say the sentence. Get ready. (Signal.) *It is hot.*

b. Now you're going to say it the slow way. Get ready. (Signal for each word as the children say) *It* (pause) *is* (pause) *hot.* (Repeat until firm.)

c. Everybody, write the sentence. Spell each word the right way. ✓

END OF SPELLING LESSON 79

Lesson 80

WORD WRITING

EXERCISE 1

Write sound combination words **far, farm**

a. (Write on the board: **far, farm.**)

b. (Point to **far.**) Everybody, read this word the fast way. Get ready. (Signal.) *Far.* Yes, **far.**

c. Everybody, say the sounds you write for the word (pause) **far.** Get ready. (Touch **f, ar** as the children say) *fff* (pause) *ar.* (Repeat until firm.)

d. (Erase **far.**) Everybody, write the word (pause) **far.** ✓

e. (Repeat *b* through *d* for **farm.**)

EXERCISE 2

Children write **can**

You're going to write the word **can.** Think about the sounds in (pause) **can** and write the word. ✓

> **To correct**
> 1. Say the sounds in **can.** (Signal.) *Caaannn.*
> 2. Say the sounds the hard way. (Signal.) *C* (pause) *aaa* (pause) *nnn.*
> 3. Write the word **can.** ✓

EXERCISE 3

Children write **me, sand, hid**

a. You're going to write the word **me.** Think about the sounds in (pause) **me** and write the word. ✓

b. (Repeat *a* for **sand, hid.**)

SENTENCE WRITING

EXERCISE 4

Children write a sentence

a. Listen to this sentence. **He had a fan.** Your turn. Say the sentence. Get ready. (Signal.) *He had a fan.*

b. Now you're going to say it the slow way. Get ready. (Signal for each word as the children say) *He* (pause) *had* (pause) *a* (pause) *fan.* (Repeat until firm.)

c. Everybody, write the sentence. Spell each word the right way. ✓

END OF SPELLING LESSON 80

Lesson 81

WORD WRITING

Children write **and, mud, hot, can**

a. You're going to write the word **and.** Think about the sounds in (pause) **and** and write the word. ✓

> **To correct**
> 1. Say the sounds in **and.** (Signal.) *Aaannnd.*
> 2. Say the sounds the hard way. (Signal.) *Aaa* (pause) *nnn* (pause) *d.*
> 3. Write the word **and.** ✓

b. (Repeat *a* for **mud, hot, can.**)

EXERCISE 2

Write sound combination words **far, bar, farm, barn**

a. (Write on the board: **far, bar, farm, barn.**)
b. (Point to **far.**) Everybody, read this word the fast way. Get ready. (Signal.) *Far.* Yes, **far.**
c. Everybody, say the sounds you write for the word (pause) **far.** Get ready. (Touch **f, ar** as the children say) *fff* (pause) *ar.* (Repeat until firm.)

d. (Erase **far.**) Everybody, write the word (pause) **far.** ✓
e. (Repeat *b* through *d* for **bar, farm, barn.**)

EXERCISE 3

Children write **arm**

a. You're going to write the word (pause) **arm.** Say the sounds you write for (pause) **arm.** Get ready. (Signal for each sound as the children say) *ar* (pause) *mmm.* (The children are to pause between the sounds. Repeat until firm.)
b. Everybody, write the word (pause) **arm.** ✓

EXERCISE 4

Children write **car**

a. You're going to write the word (pause) **car.** When you write the word (pause) **car,** you write these sounds. **C** (pause) **ar.**
b. Say the sounds you write for (pause) **car.** (Signal for each sound as the children say) *c* (pause) *ar.* (The children are to pause between sounds. Repeat until firm.)
c. Everybody, write the word (pause) **car.** ✓

SENTENCE WRITING

EXERCISE 5

Children write a sentence

a. Listen to this sentence. **His dad is sad.** Your turn. Say the sentence. Get ready. (Signal.) *His dad is sad.*
b. Now you're going to say it the slow way. Get ready. (Signal for each word as the children say) *His* (pause) *dad* (pause) *is* (pause) *sad.* (Repeat until firm.)
c. Everybody, write the sentence. Spell each word the right way. ✓

END OF SPELLING LESSON 81

Lesson 82

WORD WRITING

EXERCISE 1

Children write **car, far**

a. You're going to write the word (pause) **car.** Say the sounds you write for (pause) **car.** (Signal for each sound as the children say) *c* (pause) *ar.* (The children are to pause between sounds. Repeat until firm.)
b. Everybody, write the word (pause) **car.** ✓

c. Now you're going to write the word (pause) **far.** Say the sounds you write for (pause) **far.** (Signal for each sound as the children say) *fff* (pause) *ar.* (The children are to pause between sounds. Repeat until firm.)

d. Everybody, write the word (pause) **far.** ✓

EXERCISE 2

Children write **arm, farm**

a. You're going to write the word **arm.** Think about the sounds in (pause) **arm** and write the word. ✓

> **To correct**
> 1. Say the sounds the hard way. (Signal.) *Ar* (pause) *mmm.*
> 2. Write the word **arm.** ✓

b. (Repeat *a* for **farm.**)

SENTENCE WRITING

EXERCISE 3

Children write a sentence

a. Listen to this sentence. **His dad has sand.** Your turn. Say that sentence. Get ready. (Signal.) *His dad has sand.*

b. Now you're going to say it the slow way. Get ready. (Signal for each word as the children say) *His* (pause) *dad* (pause) *has* (pause) *sand.* (Repeat until firm.)

---

c. Everybody, write the sentence. Spell each word the right way. ✓

END OF SPELLING LESSON 82

Lesson 83

WORD WRITING

EXERCISE 1

Children write **are**

a. You're going to write the word (pause) **are.** When you write the word (pause) **are,** you write these sounds. **Ar** (pause) *ēēē.*

b. Say the sounds you write for (pause) **are.** (Signal for each sound as the children say) *ar* (pause) *ēēē.* (The children are to pause between sounds. Repeat until firm.)

c. Everybody, write the word (pause) **are.** ✓

EXERCISE 2

Children write **far, car**

a. You're going to write the word (pause) **far.** Say the sounds you write for (pause) **far.** Get ready. (Signal for each sound as the children say) *fff* (pause) *ar.* (The children are to pause between the sounds. Repeat until firm.)

---

b. Everybody, write the word (pause) **far.** ✓

c. Now you're going to write the word (pause) **car.** Say the sounds you write for (pause) **car.** (Signal for each sound as the children say) *c* (pause) *ar.* (The children are to pause between sounds. Repeat until firm.)

d. Everybody, write the word (pause) **car.** ✓

EXERCISE 3

Children write **not, land, ant, hand**

a. You're going to write the word **not.** Think about the sounds in (pause) **not** and write the word. ✓

> **To correct**
> 1. Say the sounds in **not.** (Signal.) *Nnnooot.*
> 2. Say the sounds the hard way. (Signal.) *Nnn* (pause) *ooo* (pause) *t.*
> 3. Write the word **not.** ✓

b. (Repeat *a* for **land, ant, hand.**)

SENTENCE WRITING

EXERCISE 4

Children write a sentence

a. Listen to this sentence. **He has a dad.** Your turn. Say that sentence. Get ready. (Signal.) *He has a dad.*

b. Now you're going to say it the slow way. Get ready. (Signal for each word as the children say) *He* (pause) *has* (pause) *a* (pause) *dad.* (Repeat until firm.)

c. Everybody, write the sentence. Spell each word the right way. ✓

END OF SPELLING LESSON 83

Lesson 84

WORD WRITING

EXERCISE 1

Children write **car**

a. You're going to write the word (pause) **car.** Say the sounds you write for (pause) **car.** Get ready. (Signal for each sound as the children say) *c* (pause) *ar.* (The children are to pause between the sounds. Repeat until firm.)

b. Everybody, write the word (pause) **car.** ✓

EXERCISE 2

Children write **tan, man**

a. You're going to write the word **tan.** Think about the sounds in (pause) **tan** and write the word. ✓

To correct

1. Say the sounds in **tan.** (Signal.) *Taaannn.*
2. Say the sounds the hard way. (Signal.) *T* (pause) *aaa* (pause) *nnn.*
3. Write the word **tan.** ✓

b. (Repeat *a* for **man.**)

EXERCISE 3

Children write **are**

a. You're going to write the word (pause) **are.** When you write the word (pause) **are,** you write these sounds. **Ar** (pause) *ēēē.*

b. Say the sounds you write for (pause) **are.** (Signal for each sound as the children say) *ar* (pause) *ēēē.* (The children are to pause between sounds. Repeat until firm.)

c. Write the word (pause) **are.** ✓

EXERCISE 4

Children write **was, can, is**

a. You're going to write the word **was.** Think about the sounds in (pause) **was** and write the word. ✓

To correct

1. Say the sounds the hard way. (Signal.) *Www* (pause) *aaa* (pause) *sss.*
2. Write the word **was.** ✓

b. (Repeat *a* for **can, is.**)

EXERCISE 5

Children write **far**

a. You're going to write the word (pause) **far.** Say the sounds you write for (pause) **far.** Get ready. (Signal for each sound as the children say) *fff* (pause) *ar.* (The children are to pause between the sounds. Repeat until firm.)

b. Everybody, write the word (pause) **far.** ✓

SENTENCE WRITING

EXERCISE 6

Children write a sentence

a. Listen to this sentence. **A farm is fun.** Your turn. Say that sentence. Get ready. (Signal.) *A farm is fun.*

b. Now you're going to say it the slow way. Get ready. (Signal for each word as the children say) *A* (pause) *farm* (pause) *is* (pause) *fun.* (Repeat until firm.)

c. Everybody, write the sentence. Spell each word the right way. ✓

END OF SPELLING LESSON 84

Lesson 85

WORD WRITING

EXERCISE 1

Children write are

a. You're going to write the word (pause) **are.** Say the sounds you write for (pause) **are.** Get ready. (Signal for each sound as the children say) *ar* (pause) *ēēē.* (The children are to pause between the sounds. Repeat until firm.)
b. Everybody, write the word (pause) **are.** ✓

EXERCISE 2

Children write car

a. You're going to write the word (pause) **car.** Say the sounds you write for (pause) **car.** Get ready. (Signal for each sound as the children say) *c* (pause) *ar.* (The children are to pause between the sounds. Repeat until firm.)
b. Everybody, write the word (pause) **car.** ✓

EXERCISE 3

Children write card, hard

a. You're going to write the word (pause) **card.** When you write the word (pause) **card,** you write these sounds. **C** (pause) **ar** (pause) **d.**

b. Say the sounds you write for (pause) **card.** (Signal for each sound as the children say) *c* (pause) *ar* (pause) *d.* (The children are to pause between the sounds. Repeat until firm.)
c. Everybody, write the word (pause) **card.** ✓
d. (Repeat *a* through *c* for **hard.**)

EXERCISE 4

Children write nod, rod

a. You're going to write the word **nod.** Think about the sounds in (pause) **nod** and write the word. ✓

> **To correct**
> 1. Say the sounds in **nod.** (Signal.) *Nnnoood.*
> 2. Say the sounds the hard way. (Signal.) *Nnn* (pause) *ooo* (pause) *d.*
> 3. Write the word **nod.** ✓

b. (Repeat *a* for **rod.**)

SENTENCE WRITING

EXERCISE 5

Children write a sentence

a. Listen to this sentence. **I am not sad.** Your turn. Say that sentence. Get ready. (Signal.) *I am not sad.*

b. Now you're going to say it the slow way. Get ready. (Signal for each word as the children say) *I* (pause) *am* (pause) *not* (pause) *sad.* (Repeat until firm.)
c. Everybody, write the sentence. Spell each word the right way. ✓

END OF SPELLING LESSON 85

Lesson 86

WORD WRITING

EXERCISE 1

Children write we, hid

a. You're going to write the word **we.** Think about the sounds in (pause) **we** and write the word. ✓

> **To correct**
> 1. Say the sounds in **we.** (Signal.) *Wwwēēē.*
> 2. Say the sounds the hard way. (Signal.) *Www* (pause) *ēēē.*
> 3. Write the word **we.** ✓

b. (Repeat *a* for **hid.**)

EXERCISE 2

Children write **are**

a. You're going to write the word (pause) **are.** Say the sounds you write for (pause) **are.** Get ready. (Signal for each sound as the children say) *ar* (pause) *ēēē*. (The children are to pause between the sounds. Repeat until firm.)

b. Everybody, write the word (pause) **are.** ✓

EXERCISE 3

Children write **was, has, can**

a. You're going to write the word **was.** Think about the sounds in (pause) **was** and write the word. ✓

> **To correct**
> 1. Say the sounds the hard way. (Signal.) *Www* (pause) *aaa* (pause) *sss*.
> 2. Write the word **was.** ✓

b. (Repeat *a* for **has, can.**)

SENTENCE WRITING

EXERCISE 4

Children write a sentence

a. Listen to this sentence. **His dad was mad.** Your turn. Say that sentence. Get ready. (Signal.) *His dad was mad.*

b. Now you're going to say it the slow way. Get ready. (Signal for each word as the children say) *His* (pause) *dad* (pause) *was* (pause) *mad*. (Repeat until firm.)

c. Everybody, write the sentence. Spell each word the right way. ✓

END OF SPELLING LESSON 86

Lesson 87

WORD WRITING

EXERCISE 1

Children write **are, sit**

a. You're going to write the word **are.** Think about the sounds in (pause) **are** and write the word. ✓

> **To correct**
> 1. Say the sounds the hard way. (Signal.) *Ar* (pause) *ēēē*.
> 2. Write the word **are.** ✓

b. (Repeat *a* for **sit.**)

EXERCISE 2

Children write **bit**

a. You're going to write the word (pause) **bit.** This word rhymes with **sit.** I'll say the sounds in (pause) **bit** the hard way. Listen. **B** (pause) **iii** (pause) **t.**

b. Your turn. Say the sounds in (pause) **bit.** Get ready. (Signal for each sound as the children say) *b* (pause) *iii* (pause) *t*. (The children are to pause between sounds. Repeat until firm.)

c. Everybody, write the word (pause) **bit.** ✓

EXERCISE 3

Children write **land, sand**

a. You're going to write the word **land.** Think about the sounds in (pause) **land** and write the word. ✓

b. (Repeat *a* for **sand.**)

EXERCISE 4

Children write **card**

a. You're going to write the word (pause) **card.** Say the sounds you write for (pause) **card.** Get ready. (Signal for each sound as the children say) *c* (pause) *ar* (pause) *d*. (The children are to pause between the sounds. Repeat until firm.)

b. Everybody, write the word (pause) **card.** ✓

Children write **cat**

a. You're going to write the word **cat.** Listen. **Cat.** Saying the sounds in (pause) **cat** the hard way. Get ready. (Signal for each sound as the children say) *c* (pause) *aaa* (pause) *t.* (The children are to pause between the sounds. Repeat until firm.)

b. Everybody, write the word (pause) **cat.** ✓

SENTENCE WRITING

Children write a sentence

a. Listen to this sentence. **I am not fat.** Your turn. Say that sentence. Get ready. (Signal.) *I am not fat.*

b. Now you're going to say it the slow way. Get ready. (Signal for each word as the children say) *I* (pause) *am* (pause) *not* (pause) *fat.* (Repeat until firm.)

c. Everybody, write the sentence. Spell each word the right way. ✓

END OF SPELLING LESSON 87

Lesson 88

WORD WRITING

Children write **card, farm, is**

a. You're going to write the word **card.** Think about the sounds in (pause) **card** and write the word. ✓

> **To correct**
> 1. Say the sounds the hard way. (Signal.) *C* (pause) *ar* (pause) *d.*
> 2. Write the word **card.** ✓

b. (Repeat *a* for **farm, is.**)

Children write **bit**

a. You're going to write the word (pause) **bit.** This word rhymes with **sit.** I'll say the sounds in (pause) **bit** the hard way. Listen. **B** (pause) **iii** (pause) **t.**

b. Your turn. Say the sounds in (pause) **bit.** Get ready. (Signal for each sound as the children say) *b* (pause) *iii* (pause) *t.* (The children are to pause between the sounds. Repeat until firm.)

c. Everybody, write the word (pause) **bit.** ✓

Children write **not, hot**

a. You're going to write the word **not.** Think about the sounds in (pause) **not** and write the word. ✓

> **To correct**
> 1. Say the sounds in **not.** (Signal.) *Nnnooot.*
> 2. Say the sounds the hard way. (Signal.) *Nnn* (pause) *ooo* (pause) *t.*
> 3. Write the word **not.** ✓

b. (Repeat *a* for **hot.**)

SENTENCE WRITING

Children write a sentence

a. Listen to this sentence. **He did run far.** Your turn. Say that sentence. Get ready. (Signal.) *He did run far.*

b. Now you're going to say it the slow way. Get ready. (Signal for each word as the children say) *He* (pause) *did* (pause) *run* (pause) *far.* (Repeat until firm.)

c. Everybody, write the sentence. Spell each word the right way. ✓

END OF SPELLING LESSON 88

Lesson 89

WORD WRITING

EXERCISE 1

Children write bad

a. You're going to write the word (pause) **bad.** This word rhymes with **sad.** I'll say the sounds in (pause) **bad** the hard way. Listen. **B** (pause) **aaa** (pause) **d.**

b. Your turn. Say the sounds in (pause) **bad.** Get ready. (Signal for each sound as the children say) *b* (pause) *aaa* (pause) *d.* (The children are to pause between the sounds. Repeat until firm.)

c. Everybody, write the word (pause) **bad.** ✓

EXERCISE 2

Children write hard, his, card

a. You're going to write the word **hard.** Think about the sounds in (pause) **hard** and write the word. ✓

> **To correct**
> 1. Say the sounds the hard way. (Signal.) *H* (pause) *ar* (pause) *d.*
> 2. Write the word **hard.** ✓

b. (Repeat *a* for **his, card.**)

EXERCISE 3

Children write cart

a. You're going to write the word (pause) **cart.** Say the sounds you write for (pause) **cart.** Get ready. (Signal for each sound as the children say) *c* (pause) *ar* (pause) *t.* (The children are to pause between the sounds. Repeat until firm.)

b. Everybody, write the word (pause) **cart.** ✓

EXERCISE 4

Children write cat

a. You're going to write the word **cat.** Listen. **Cat.** Saying the sounds in (pause) **cat** the hard way. Get ready. (Signal for each sound as the children say) *c* (pause) *aaa* (pause) *t.* (The children are to pause between the sounds. Repeat until firm.)

b. Everybody, write the word (pause) **cat.** ✓

SENTENCE WRITING

EXERCISE 5

Children write a sentence

a. Listen to this sentence. **We are not sad.** Your turn. Say that sentence. Get ready. (Signal.) *We are not sad.*

b. Now you're going to say it the slow way. Get ready. (Signal for each word as the children say) *we* (pause) *are* (pause) *not* (pause) *sad.* (Repeat until firm.)

c. Everybody, write the sentence. Spell each word the right way. ✓

END OF SPELLING LESSON 89

Lesson 90

WORD WRITING

EXERCISE 1

Children write was, can

a. You're going to write the word **was.** Think about the sounds in (pause) **was** and write the word. ✓

> **To correct**
> 1. Say the sounds the hard way. (Signal.) *Www* (pause) *aaa* (pause) *sss.*
> 2. Write the word **was.** ✓

b. You're going to write the word **can.** Think about the sounds in (pause) **can** and write the word. ✓

To correct

1. Say the sounds in **can.** (Signal.) *Caaannn.*
2. Say the sounds the hard way. (Signal.) *C* (pause) *aaa* (pause) *nnn.*
3. Write the word **can.** ✓

Children write **cat**

a. You're going to write the word **cat.** Listen. **Cat.** Saying the sounds in (pause) **cat** the hard way. Get ready. (Signal for each sound as the children say) *c* (pause) *aaa* (pause) *t.* (The children are to pause between the sounds. Repeat until firm.)
b. Everybody, write the word (pause) **cat.** ✓

EXERCISE 3

Children write **see**

a. You're going to write the word (pause) **see.** When you write the word (pause) **see,** you write these sounds. **Sss** (pause) *ēēē* (pause) *ēēē.*
b. Say the sounds you write for (pause) **see.** (Signal for each sound as the children say) *sss* (pause) *ēēē* (pause) *ēēē.* (The children are to pause between sounds. Repeat until firm.)
c. Write the word (pause) **see.** ✓

EXERCISE 4

Children write **farm**

You're going to write the word **farm.** Think about the sounds in (pause) **farm** and write the word. ✓

EXERCISE 5

Children write **but**

a. You're going to write the word (pause) **but.** This word is tough. I'll say the sounds in (pause) **but** the hard way. Listen. **B** (pause) **uuu** (pause) **t.**
b. Your turn. Say the sounds in (pause) **but.** Get ready. (Signal for each sound as the children say) *b* (pause) *uuu* (pause) *t.* (The children are to pause between sounds. Repeat until firm.)
c. Everybody, write the word (pause) **but.** ✓

SENTENCE WRITING

EXERCISE 6

Children write a sentence

a. Listen to this sentence. **I am in mud.** Your turn. Say that sentence. Get ready. (Signal.) *I am in mud.*
b. Now you're going to say it the slow way. Get ready. (Signal for each word as the children say) *I* (pause) *am* (pause) *in* (pause) *mud.* (Repeat until firm.)

c. Everybody, write the sentence. Spell each word the right way. ✓

END OF SPELLING LESSON 90

Lesson 91

WORD WRITING

EXERCISE 1

Children write **see**

a. You're going to write the word (pause) **see.** When you write the word (pause) **see,** you write these sounds. **Sss** (pause) *ēēē* (pause) *ēēē.*
b. Say the sounds you write for (pause) **see.** (Signal for each sound as the children say) *sss* (pause) *ēēē* (pause) *ēēē.* (The children are to pause between sounds. Repeat until firm.)
c. Write the word (pause) **see.** ✓

EXERCISE 2

Children write **but**

a. You're going to write the word (pause) **but.** This word rhymes with **hut.** I'll say the sounds in (pause) **but** the hard way. Listen. **B** (pause) **uuu** (pause) **t.**

b. Your turn. Say the sounds in (pause) **but.** Get ready. (Signal for each sound as the children say) *b* (pause) *uuu* (pause) *t.* (The children are to pause between the sounds. Repeat until firm.)

c. Everybody, write the word (pause) **but.** ✓

Children write **his**

You're going to write the word **his.** Think about the sounds in (pause) **his** and write the word. ✓

> **To correct**
> 1. Say the sounds the hard way. (Signal.) *H* (pause) *iii* (pause) *sss.*
> 2. Write the word **his.** ✓

Children write **bit**

a. You're going to write the word **bit.** Listen. **Bit.** Saying the sounds in (pause) **bit** the hard way. Get ready. (Signal for each sound as the children say) *b* (pause) *iii* (pause) *t.* (The children are to pause between the sounds. Repeat until firm.)

b. Everybody, write the word (pause) **bit.** ✓

SENTENCE WRITING

Children write a sentence

a. Listen to this sentence. **We are in sand.** Your turn. Say the sentence. Get ready. (Signal.) *We are in sand.*

b. Now you're going to say it the slow way. Get ready. (Signal for each word as the children say) *we* (pause) *are* (pause) *in* (pause) *sand.* (Repeat until firm.)

c. Everybody, write the sentence. Spell each word the right way. ✓

END OF SPELLING LESSON 91

Lesson 92

WORD WRITING

Children write **bad**

a. You're going to write the word (pause) **bad.** Say the sounds you write for (pause) **bad.** Get ready. (Signal for each sound as the children say) *b* (pause) *aaa* (pause) *d.* (The children are to pause between the sounds. Repeat until firm.)

b. Everybody, write the word (pause) **bad.** ✓

Children write **see**

a. You're going to write the word (pause) **see.** When you write the word (pause) **see,** you write these sounds. **Sss** (pause) ēēē (pause) ēēē.

b. Say the sounds you write for (pause) **see.** (Signal for each sound as the children say) *sss* (pause) *ēēē* (pause) *ēēē.* (The children are to pause between sounds. Repeat until firm.)

c. Write the word (pause) **see.** ✓

Children write **but**

a. You're going to write the word (pause) **but.** Say the sounds you write for (pause) **but.** Get ready. (Signal for each sound as the children say) *b* (pause) *uuu* (pause) *t.* (The children are to pause between the sounds. Repeat until firm.)

b. Everybody, write the word (pause) **but.** ✓

Children write **and, are**

a. You're going to write the word **and.** Think about the sounds in (pause) **and** and write the word. ✓

b. (Repeat *a* for **are.**)

Children write **bit**

a. You're going to write the word (pause) **bit.** Say the sounds you write for (pause) **bit.** Get ready. (Signal for each sound as the children say) *b* (pause) *iii* (pause) *t.* (The children are to pause between the sounds. Repeat until firm.)

b. Everybody, write the word (pause) **bit.** ✓

SENTENCE WRITING

Children write a sentence

a. Listen to this sentence. **We are on land.** Your turn. Say that sentence. Get ready. (Signal.) *We are on land.*

b. Now you're going to say it the slow way. Get ready. (Signal for each word as the children say) *We* (pause) *are* (pause) *on* (pause) *land.* (Repeat until firm.)

c. Everybody, write the sentence. Spell each word the right way. ✓

END OF SPELLING LESSON 92

Lesson 93

SOUND WRITING

Introduce sound combination **th**

a. (Write on the board: **th.**)

b. (Point to **th.**) Everybody, tell me the sound these letters make. Get ready. (Signal.) *ththth. Yes,* *ththth.*

c. (Erase **th.**) Everybody, write the letters that go together and make the sound. **th.** ✓

WORD WRITING

Children write **bit**

You're going to write the word **bit.** Think about the sounds in (pause) **bit** and write the word. ✓

To correct
1. Say the sounds in **bit.** (Signal.) *Biiit.*
2. Say the sounds the hard way. (Signal.) *B* (pause) *iii* (pause) *t.*
3. Write the word **bit.** ✓

Children write **see**

a. You're going to write the word (pause) **see.** Say the sounds you write for (pause) **see.** Get ready. (Signal for each sound as the children say) *sss* (pause) *ēēē* (pause) *ēēē.* (The children are to pause between the sounds. Repeat until firm.)

b. Everybody, write the word (pause) **see.** ✓

Children write **can, but, card**

a. You're going to write the word **can.** Think about the sounds in (pause) **can** and write the word. ✓

b. (Repeat *a* for **but.**)

c. You're going to write the word **card.** Think about the sounds in (pause) **card** and write the word. ✓

To correct
1. Say the sounds the hard way. (Signal.) *C* (pause) *ar* (pause) *d.*
2. Write the word **card.** ✓

SENTENCE WRITING

EXERCISE 5

Children write a sentence

a. Listen to this sentence. **We had a car.** Your turn. Say that sentence. Get ready. (Signal.) *We had a car.*

b. Now you're going to say it the slow way. Get ready. (Signal for each word as the children say) *we* (pause) *had* (pause) *a* (pause) *car.* (Repeat until firm.)

c. Everybody, write the sentence. Spell each word the right way. ✓

END OF SPELLING LESSON 93

Lesson 94

SOUND WRITING

EXERCISE 1

Reinforce sound combination th

a. (Write on the board: **th.**)

b. (Point to **th.**) Everybody, tell me the sound these letters make. Get ready. (Signal.) *ththth.* Yes, **ththth.**

c. (Erase **th.**) Everybody, write the letters that go together and make the sound **th.** ✓

WORD WRITING

EXERCISE 2

Children write are, bad

a. You're going to write the word **are.** Think about the sounds in (pause) **are** and write the word. ✓

> **To correct**
> 1. Say the sounds the hard way. (Signal.) *Ar* (pause) *ēēē.*
> 2. Write the word **are.** ✓

b. (Repeat *a* for **bad.**)

EXERCISE 3

Children write the

a. You're going to write the word (pause) **thē.** This word rhymes with **me.** I'll say the sounds in (pause) **thē** the hard way. Listen. **Ththth** (pause) *ēēē.*

b. Your turn. Say the sounds in (pause) **thē.** Get ready. (Signal for each sound as the children say) *ththth* (pause) *ēēē.* (The children are to pause between the sounds. Repeat until firm.)

c. Everybody, write the word (pause) **thē.** ✓ (Accept **the** not **thē.**)

SENTENCE WRITING

EXERCISE 4

Children write a sentence

a. Listen to this sentence. **He has a farm.** Your turn. Say that sentence. Get ready. (Signal.) *He has a farm.*

b. Now you're going to say it the slow way. Get ready. (Signal for each word as the children say) *he* (pause) *has* (pause) *a* (pause) *farm.* (Repeat until firm.)

c. Everybody, write the sentence. Spell each word the right way. ✓

END OF SPELLING LESSON 94

Lesson 95

WORD WRITING

EXERCISE 1

Write sound combination words this, that, then, them

a. (Write on the board: **this, that, then, them.**)

b. (Point to **this.**) Everybody, read this word the fast way. Get ready. (Signal.) *This.* Yes, **this.**

c. Everybody, say the sounds you write for the word (pause) **this.** Get ready. (Touch **th, i, s** as the children say) *ththth* (pause) *iii* (pause) *sss.* (Repeat until firm.)

d. (Erase **this.**) Everybody, write the word (pause) **this.** ✓

e. (Point to **that.**) Everybody, read this word the fast way. Get ready. (Signal.) *That.* Yes, **that.**

f. Everybody, say the sounds you write for the word (pause) **that.** Get ready. (Touch **th, a, t** as the children say) *ththth* (pause) *aaa* (pause) *t.* (Repeat until firm.)

g. (Erase **that.**) Everybody, write the word (pause) **that.** ✓

h. (Point to **then.**) Everybody, read this word the fast way. Get ready. (Signal.) *Then.* Yes, **then.**

i. Everybody, say the sounds you write for the word (pause) **then.** Get ready. (Touch **th, e, n** as the children say) *ththth* (pause) *eee* (pause) *nnn.* (Repeat until firm.)

j. (Erase **then.**) Everybody, write the word (pause) **then.** ✓

k. (Point to **them.**) Everybody, read this word the fast way. Get ready. (Signal.) *Them.* Yes, **them.**

l. Everybody, say the sounds you write for the word (pause) **them.** Get ready. (Touch **th, e, m** as the children say) *ththth* (pause) *eee* (pause) *mmm.* (Repeat until firm.)

m. (Erase **them.**) Everybody, write the word (pause) **them.** ✓

EXERCISE 2

Children write **see**

a. You're going to write the word (pause) **see.** Say the sounds you write for (pause) **see.** Get ready. (Signal for each sound as the children say) *sss* (pause) *ēēē* (pause) *ēēē.* (The children are to pause between the sounds. Repeat until firm.)

b. Everybody, write the word (pause) **see.** ✓

EXERCISE 3

Children write **the**

a. You're going to write the word **thē.** Listen. **Thē.** Saying the sounds in (pause) **thē** the hard way. Get ready. (Signal for each sound as the children say) *ththth* (pause) *ēēē.* (The children are to pause between the sounds. Repeat until firm.)

b. Everybody, write the word (pause) **thē.** ✓
(Accept **the** not **thē.**)

EXERCISE 4

Children write **are**

You're going to write the word **are.** Think about the sounds in (pause) **are** and write the word. ✓

To correct
1. Say the sounds the hard way. (Signal.) *Ar* (pause) *ēēē.*
2. Write the word **are.** ✓

EXERCISE 5

Children write **this, them**

a. You're going to write the word **this.** Listen. **This.** Saying the sounds in (pause) **this** the hard way. Get ready. (Signal for each sound as the children say) *ththth* (pause) *iii* (pause) *sss.* (The children are to pause between the sounds. Repeat until firm.)

b. Everybody, write the word (pause) **this.** ✓

c. (Repeat *a* and *b* for **them.**)

SENTENCE WRITING

EXERCISE 6

Children write a sentence

a. Listen to this sentence. **He did not run.** Your turn. Say that sentence. Get ready. (Signal.) *He did not run.*

b. Now you're going to say it the slow way. Get ready. (Signal for each word as the children say) *he* (pause) *did* (pause) *not* (pause) *run.* (Repeat until firm.)

c. Everybody, write the sentence. Spell each word the right way. ✓

END OF SPELLING LESSON 95

Lesson 96

WORD WRITING

Write sound combination words that, then, this, them

a. (Write on the board: **that, then, this, them.**)

b. (Point to **that.**) Everybody, read this word the fast way. Get ready. (Signal.) *That.* Yes, **that.**

c. Everybody, say the sounds you write for the word (pause) **that.** Get ready. (Touch **th, a, t** as the children say) *ththth* (pause) *aaa* (pause) *t.* (Repeat until firm.)

d. (Erase **that.**) Everybody, write the word (pause) **that.** ✓

e. (Point to **then.**) Everybody, read this word the fast way. Get ready. (Signal.) *Then.* Yes, **then.**

f. Everybody, say the sounds you write for the word (pause) **then.** Get ready. (Touch **th, e, n** as the children say) *ththth* (pause) *eee* (pause) *nnn.* (Repeat until firm.)

g. (Erase **then.**) Everybody, write the word (pause) **then.** ✓

h. (Point to **this.**) Everybody, read this word the fast way. Get ready. (Signal.) *This.* Yes, **this.**

i. Everybody, say the sounds you write for the word (pause) **this.** Get ready. (Touch **th, i, s** as the children say) *ththth* (pause) *iii* (pause) *sss.* (Repeat until firm.)

j. (Erase **this.**) Everybody, write the word (pause) **this.** ✓

k. (Point to **them.**) Everybody, read this word the fast way. Get ready. (Signal.) *Them.* Yes, **them.**

l. Everybody, say the sounds you write for the word (pause) **them.** Get ready. (Touch **th, e, m** as the children say) *ththth* (pause) *eee* (pause) *mmm.* (Repeat until firm.)

m. (Erase **them.**) Everybody, write the word (pause) **them.** ✓

Children write will

Note: Double letters are sounded out twice in Spelling lessons only.

a. You're going to write the word (pause) **will.** When you write the word (pause) **will,** you write these sounds. **Www** (pause) **iii** (pause) **lll** (pause) **lll.**

b. Say the sounds you write for (pause) **will.** (Signal for each sound as the children say) *www* (pause) *iii* (pause) *lll* (pause) *lll.* (The children are to pause between sounds. Repeat until firm.)

c. Everybody, write the word (pause) **will.** ✓

Children write arm

You're going to write the word **arm.** Think about the sounds in (pause) **arm** and write the word. ✓

> **To correct**
> 1. Say the sounds the hard way. (Signal.) *Ar* (pause) *mmm.*
> 2. Write the word **arm.** ✓

Children write barn

a. You're going to write the word (pause) **barn.** When you write the word (pause) **barn,** you write these sounds. **B** (pause) **ar** (pause) **nnn.**

b. Say the sounds you write for (pause) **barn.** (Signal for each sound as the children say) *b* (pause) *ar* (pause) *nnn.* (The children are to pause between sounds. Repeat until firm.)

c. Everybody, write the word (pause) **barn.** ✓

Children write **that**

a. You're going to write the word **that**. Listen. **That**. Saying the sounds in (pause) **that** the hard way. Get ready. (Signal for each sound as the children say) *ththth* (pause) *aaa* (pause) *t.* (The children are to pause between the sounds. Repeat until firm.)

b. Everybody, write the word (pause) **that**. ✓

Children write **can**

You're going to write the word **can**. Think about the sounds in (pause) **can** and write the word. ✓

SENTENCE WRITING

Children write a sentence

a. Listen to this sentence. **We are in the sand.** Your turn. Say that sentence. Get ready. (Signal.) *We are in the sand.*

b. Now you're going to say it the slow way. Get ready. (Signal for each word as the children say) *We* (pause) *are* (pause) *in* (pause) *the* (pause) *sand.* (Repeat until firm.)

c. Everybody, write the sentence. Spell each word the right way. ✓

END OF SPELLING LESSON 96

Lesson 97

WORD WRITING

Write sound combination words **them, this, that, then**

a. (Write on the board: **them, this, that, the.**)

b. (Point to **them.**) Everybody, read this word the fast way. Get ready. (Signal.) *Them.* Yes, **them.**

c. Everybody, say the sounds you write for the word (pause) **them.** Get ready. (Touch **th, e, m** as the children say) *ththth* (pause) *eee* (pause) *mmm.* (Repeat until firm.)

d. (Erase **them.**) Everybody, write the word (pause) **them.** ✓

e. (Repeat *b* through *d* for **this, that, then.**)

Children write **see**

a. You're going to write the word (pause) **see.** Say the sounds you write for (pause) **see.** Get ready. (Signal for each sound as the children say) *sss* (pause) *ēēē* (pause) *ēēē.* (The children are to pause between the sounds. Repeat until firm.)

b. Everybody, write the word (pause) **see.** ✓

Children write **this**

a. You're going to write the word **this.** Think about the sounds in (pause) **this** and write the word. ✓

> **To correct**
> 1. Say the sounds in **this.** (Signal.) *Thththiiisss.*
> 2. Say the sounds the hard way. (Signal.) *Thththth* (pause) *iii* (pause) *sss.*
> 3. Write the word **this.** ✓

Children write **will**

a. You're going to write the word (pause) **will.** When you write the word (pause) **will,** you write these sounds. **Www** (pause) **iii** (pause) **lll** (pause) **lll.**

b. Say the sounds you write for (pause) **will.** (Signal for each sound as the children say) *www* (pause) *iii* (pause) *lll* (pause) *lll.* (The children are to pause between the sounds. Repeat until firm.)

c. Everybody, write the word (pause) **will.** ✓

Children write **barn**

a. You're going to write the word (pause) **barn.** Say the sounds you write for (pause) **barn.** Get ready. (Signal for each sound as the children say) *b* (pause) *ar* (pause) *nnn.* (The children are to pause between the sounds. Repeat until firm.)

b. Everybody, write the word (pause) **barn.** ✓

Children write **the, cat**

a. You're going to write the word **thē.** Think about the sounds in (pause) **thē** and write the word. ✓

> **To correct**
> 1. Say the sounds in **thē.** (Signal.) *Thththēēē.*
> 2. Say the sounds the hard way. (Signal.) *Thththth* (pause) *ēēē.*
> 3. Write the word **thē.** ✓

b. (Repeat *a* for **cat.**)

SENTENCE WRITING

Children write a sentence

a. Listen to this sentence. **The ant was bad.** Your turn. Say that sentence. Get ready. (Signal.) *The ant was bad.*

b. Now you're going to say it the slow way. Get ready. (Signal for each word as the children say) *The* (pause) *ant* (pause) *was* (pause) *bad.* (Repeat until firm.)

c. Everybody, write the sentence. Spell each word the right way. ✓

END OF SPELLING LESSON 97

Lesson 98

WORD WRITING

Children write **but, that, cat**

a. You're going to write the word **but.** Think about the sounds in (pause) **but** and write the word. ✓

> **To correct**
> 1. Say the sounds in **but.** (Signal.) *Buuut.*
> 2. Say the sounds the hard way. (Signal.) *B* (pause) *uuu* (pause) *t.*
> 3. Write the word **but.** ✓

b. (Repeat *a* for **that, cat.**)

Children write **will**

a. You're going to write the word (pause) **will.** Say the sounds you write for (pause) **will.** Get ready. (Signal for each sound as the children say) *www* (pause) *iii* (pause) *lll* (pause) *lll.* (The children are to pause between the sounds. Repeat until firm.)

b. Everybody, write the word (pause) **will.** ✓

Children write **see, this**

a. You're going to write the word **see.** Think about the sounds in (pause) **see** and write the word. ✓

> **To correct**
> 1. Say the sounds the hard way. (Signal.) *Sss* (pause) *ēēē* (pause) *ēēē.*
> 2. Write the word **see.** ✓

b. (Repeat *a* for **this.**)

SENTENCE WRITING

Children write a sentence

a. Listen to this sentence. **This car is tan.** Your turn. Say that sentence. Get ready. (Signal.) *This car is tan.*

b. Now you're going to say it the slow way. Get ready. (Signal for each word as the children say) *This* (pause) *car* (pause) *is* (pause) *tan.* (Repeat until firm.)

c. Everybody, write the sentence. Spell each word the right way. ✓

END OF SPELLING LESSON 98

Lesson 99

WORD WRITING

Say the sounds, write **that, this, them**

a. You're going to write the word (pause) **that.** Say the sounds in **that.** Get ready. (Signal for each sound as the children say) *ththth* (pause) *aaa* (pause) *t.* (Repeat until firm.)

b. Everybody, write the word (pause) **that.** ✓

c. (Repeat *a* and *b* for **this, them.**)

EXERCISE 2

Children write **bill**

a. You're going to write the word (pause) **bill.** When you write the word (pause) **bill,** you write these sounds. **B** (pause) **lll** (pause) **lll.**

b. Say the sounds you write for (pause) **bill.** (Signal for each sound as the children say) *b* (pause) *iii* (pause) *lll* (pause) *lll.* (The children are to pause between the sounds. Repeat until firm.)

c. Everybody, write the word (pause) **bill.** ✓

EXERCISE 3

Children write **will**

a. You're going to write the word (pause) **will.** Say the sounds you write for (pause) **will.** Get ready. (Signal for each sound as the children say) *www* (pause) *iii* (pause) *lll* (pause) *lll.* (The children are to pause between the sounds. Repeat until firm.)

b. Everybody, write the word (pause) **will.** ✓

EXERCISE 4

Children write **are, the, but**

a. You're going to write the word **are.** Think about the sounds in (pause) **are** and write the word. ✓

To correct
1. Say the sounds the hard way. (Signal.) *Ar* (pause) *ēēē.*
2. Write the word **are.** ✓

b. You're going to write the word **the.** Think about the sounds in (pause) **the** and write the word. ✓

To correct
1. Say the sounds in **the.** (Signal.) *Thththēēē.*
2. Say the sounds the hard way. (Signal.) *Ththth* (pause) *ēēē.*
3. Write the word **the.** ✓

c. (Repeat *b* for **but.**)

SENTENCE WRITING

EXERCISE 5

Children write a sentence

a. Listen to this sentence. **It is a fat ant.** Your turn. Say that sentence. Get ready. (Signal.) *It is a fat ant.*

b. Now you're going to say it the slow way. Get ready. (Signal for each word as the children say) *it* (pause) *is* (pause) *a* (pause) *fat* (pause) *ant.* (Repeat until firm.)

c. Everybody, write the sentence. Spell each word the right way. ✓

END OF SPELLING LESSON 99

Lesson 100

WORD WRITING

EXERCISE 1

Children write see

You're going to write the word **see.** Think about the sounds in (pause) **see** and write the word. ✓

> **To correct**
> 1. Say the sounds in **see.** (Signal.) *Sssēēē.*
> 2. Say the sounds the hard way. (Signal.) *Sss* (pause) *ēēē* (pause) *ēēē.*
> 3. Write the word **see.** ✓

EXERCISE 2

Children write barn, bill, pill

a. You're going to write the word (pause) **barn.** Say the sounds you write for (pause) **barn.** Get ready. (Signal for each sound as the children say) *b* (pause) *ar* (pause) *nnn.* (The children are to pause between the sounds. Repeat until firm.)
b. Everybody, write the word (pause) **barn.** ✓

c. Now you're going to write the word (pause) **bill.** Say the sounds you write for (pause) **bill.** Get ready. (Signal for each sound as the children say) *b* (pause) *iii* (pause) *lll* (pause) *lll.* (The children are to pause between the sounds. Repeat until firm.)
d. Everybody, write the word (pause) **bill.** ✓
e. Next you're going to write the word (pause) **pill.** Say the sounds you write for (pause) **pill.** Get ready. (Signal for each sound as the children say) *p* (pause) *iii* (pause) *lll* (pause) *lll.* (The children are to pause between the sounds. Repeat until firm.)
f. Everybody, write the word (pause) **pill.** ✓

EXERCISE 3

Children write it

You're going to write the word **it.** Think about the sounds in (pause) **it** and write the word. ✓

EXERCISE 4

Children write pit

a. You're going to write the word **pit.** Listen. **Pit.** Saying the sounds in (pause) **pit** the hard way. Get ready. (Signal for each sound as the children say) *p* (pause) *iii* (pause) *t.* (The children are to pause between the sounds. Repeat until firm.)

b. Everybody, write the word (pause) **pit.** ✓

SENTENCE WRITING

EXERCISE 5

Children write a sentence

a. Listen to this sentence. **We will win a car.** Your turn. Say that sentence. Get ready. (Signal.) *We will win a car.*
b. Now you're going to say it the slow way. Get ready. (Signal for each word as the children say) *We* (pause) *will* (pause) *win* (pause) *a* (pause) *car.* (Repeat until firm.)
c. Everybody, write the sentence. Spell each word the right way. ✓

END OF SPELLING LESSON 100

Lesson 101

WORD WRITING

EXERCISE 1

Children write bar, pill, will

a. You're going to write the word (pause) **bar.** Say the sounds you write for (pause) **bar.** Get ready. (Signal for each sound as the children say) *b* (pause) *ar.* (The children are to pause between the sounds. Repeat until firm.)

b. Everybody, write the word (pause) **bar.** ✓

c. Now you're going to write the word (pause) **pill.** Say the sounds you write for (pause) **pill.** Get ready. (Signal for each sound as the children say) *p* (pause) *iii* (pause) *lll* (pause) *lll.* (The children are to pause between the sounds. Repeat until firm.)

d. Everybody, write the word (pause) **pill.** ✓

e. Next you're going to write the word (pause) **will.** Say the sounds you write for (pause) **will.** Get ready. (Signal for each sound as the children say) *www* (pause) *iii* (pause) *lll* (pause) *lll.* (The children are to pause between the sounds. Repeat until firm.)

f. Everybody, write the word (pause) **will.** ✓

Children write **ham, bit, land**

a. You're going to write the word **ham.** Think about the sounds in (pause) **ham** and write the word. ✓

To correct
1. Say the sounds in **ham.** (Signal.) *Haaammm.*
2. Say the sounds the hard way. (Signal.) *H* (pause) *aaa* (pause) *mmm.*
3. Write the word **ham.** ✓

b. (Repeat *a* for **bit, land.**)

SENTENCE WRITING

Children write a sentence

a. Listen to this sentence. **He had mud on him.** Your turn. Say that sentence. Get ready. (Signal.) *He had mud on him.*

b. Now you're going to say it the slow way. Get ready. (Signal for each word as the children say) *He* (pause) *had* (pause) *mud* (pause) *on* (pause) *him.* (Repeat until firm.)

c. Everybody, write the sentence. Spell each word the right way. ✓

END OF SPELLING LESSON 101

Lesson 102

WORD WRITING

Children write **but**

You're going to write the word **but.** Think about the sounds in (pause) **but** and write the word. ✓

To correct
1. Say the sounds in **but.** (Signal.) *Buuut.*
2. Say the sounds the hard way. (Signal.) *B* (pause) *uuu* (pause) *t.*
3. Write the word **but.** ✓

Children write **bar**

a. You're going to write the word (pause) **bar.** Say the sounds you write for (pause) **bar.** Get ready. (Signal for each sound as the children say) *b* (pause) *ar.* (The children are to pause between the sounds. Repeat until firm.)

b. Everybody, write the word (pause) **bar.** ✓

Children write **his, see, barn, and**

a. You're going to write the word **his.** Think about the sounds in (pause) **his** and write the word. ✓

To correct
1. Say the sounds the hard way. (Signal.) *H* (pause) *iii* (pause) *sss.*
2. Write the word **his.** ✓

b. You're going to write the word **see.** Think about the sounds in (pause) **see** and write the word. ✓

To correct
1. Say the sounds in **see.** (Signal.) *Sssēēē.*
2. Say the sounds the hard way. (Signal.) *Sss* (pause) *ēēē* (pause) *ēēē.*
3. Write the word **see.** ✓

c. (Repeat *b* for **barn, and.**)

SENTENCE WRITING

EXERCISE 4

Children write a sentence

a. Listen to this sentence. **We are on the farm.** Your turn. Say that sentence. Get ready. (Signal.) *We are on the farm.*

b. Now you're going to say it the slow way. Get ready. (Signal for each word as the children say) *We* (pause) *are* (pause) *on* (pause) *the* (pause) *farm.* (Repeat until firm.)

c. Everybody, write the sentence. Spell each word the right way. ✓

END OF SPELLING LESSON 102

Lesson 103

WORD WRITING

EXERCISE 1

Children write is, has, are

a. You're going to write the word (pause) **is.**

b. Say the sounds you write for (pause) **is.** Get ready. (Signal for each sound as the children say) *iii* (pause) *sss.* (Repeat until firm.)

c. Everybody, write the word (pause) **is.** ✓

d. (Repeat *a* through *c* for **has, are.**)

EXERCISE 2

Say the sounds, write if, farm, them, bat, this

a. You're going to write the word (pause) **if.** Say the sounds in **if.** Get ready. (Signal for each sound as the children say) *iii* (pause) *fff.*
(Repeat until firm.)

b. Everybody, write the word (pause) **if.** ✓

c. (Repeat *a* and *b* for **farm, them, bat, this.**)

EXERCISE 3

Write arm, car, hat, me, it, fit, we

a. You're going to write the word (pause) **arm.** Think about the sounds in **arm** and write the word. ✓

b. (Repeat *a* for **car, hat, me, it, fit, we.**)

SENTENCE WRITING

EXERCISE 4

Write one sentence

a. Listen to this sentence. **This hat will fit.** Say that sentence. Get ready. (Signal.) *This hat will fit.*

---

b. Now you're going to say that sentence the slow way. Get ready. (Signal for each word as the children say) *This* (pause) *hat* (pause) *will* (pause) *fit.*

c. Everybody, write the sentence. Spell each word the right way. Remember to put a period at the end of your sentence. ✓

END OF SPELLING LESSON 103

Lesson 104

WORD WRITING

EXERCISE 1

Say the sounds, write this, and, far, tar, barn, is, hand

a. You're going to write the word (pause) **this.** Say the sounds in **this.** Get ready. (Signal for each sound as the children say) *ththth* (pause) *iii* (pause) *sss.*
(Repeat until firm.)

b. Everybody, write the word (pause) **this.** ✓

c. (Repeat *a* and *b* for **and, far, tar, barn, is, hand.**)

Write **hat, sit, bar, it, that, me, cat, if**

a. You're going to write the word (pause) **hat.** Think about the sounds in **hat** and write the word. ✓

b. (Repeat *a* for **sit, bar, it, that, me, cat, if.**)

SENTENCE WRITING

EXERCISE 3

Write one sentence

a. Listen to this sentence. **That man will see.** Say that sentence. Get ready. (Signal.) *That man will see.*

b. Now you're going to say that sentence the slow way. Get ready. (Signal.) (Signal for each word as the children say) *That* (pause) *man* (pause) *will* (pause) *see.*

c. Everybody, write the sentence. Spell each word the right way. Remember to put a period at the end of your sentence. ✓

END OF SPELLING LESSON 104

Lesson 105

SOUND WRITING

EXERCISE 1

Introduce sound combination **sh**

a. (Write on the board: **sh.**)

b. (Point to **sh.**) Everybody, tell me the sound these letters make. Get ready. (Signal.) *shshsh.* Yes, **shshsh.**

c. (Erase **sh.**) Everybody, write the letters that go together and make the sound **sh.** ✓

WORD WRITING

EXERCISE 2

Say the sounds, write **bad, him, arm, men, ten, set**

a. You're going to write the word (pause) **bad.** Say the sounds in **bad.** Get ready. (Signal for each sound as the children say) *b* (pause) *aaa* (pause) *d.* (Repeat until firm.)

b. Everybody, write the word (pause) **bad.** ✓

c. (Repeat *a* and *b* for **him, arm, men, ten, set.**)

EXERCISE 3

Write **bar, farm, sad, has**

a. You're going to write the word (pause) **bar.** Think about the sounds in **bar** and write the word. ✓

b. (Repeat *a* for **farm, sad, has.**)

SENTENCE WRITING

EXERCISE 4

Write one sentence

a. Listen to this sentence. **He is a fat man.** Say that sentence. Get ready. (Signal.) *He is a fat man.*

b. Now you're going to say that sentence the slow way. Get ready. (Signal.) (Signal for each word as the children say) *He* (pause) *is* (pause) *a* (pause) *fat* (pause) *man.*

c. Everybody, write the sentence. Spell each word the right way. Remember to put a period at the end of your sentence. ✓

END OF SPELLING LESSON 105

Lesson 106

EXERCISE 1

Reinforce sound combination **sh**

a. (Write on the board: **sh.**)

b. (Point to **sh.**) Everybody, tell me the sound these letters make. Get ready. (Signal.) *shshsh* Yes, **shshsh.**

c. (Erase **sh.**) Everybody, write the letters that go together and make the sound **sh.** ✓

WORD WRITING

Write sound combination words she, wish, ship

a. (Write on the board: **she, wish, ship.**)
b. (Point to **she.**) Everybody, read this word the fast way. Get ready. (Signal.) *She.* Yes, **she.**
c. Everybody, say the sounds you write for the word (pause) **she.** Get ready. (Touch **sh, e** as the children say) *shshsh* (pause) *ēēē.* (Repeat until firm.)
d. (Erase **she.**) Everybody, write the word (pause) **she.** ✓
e. (Repeat *b* through *d* for **wish, ship.**)

EXERCISE 3

Say the sounds, write will, bill, pill

a. You're going to write the word (pause) **will.** Say the sounds you write for (pause) **will.** Get ready. (Signal for each sound as the children say) *www* (pause) *iii* (pause) *lll* (pause) *lll.* (Repeat until firm.)
b. Everybody, write the word (pause) **will.** ✓
c. (Repeat *a* and *b* for **bill, pill.**)

EXERCISE 4

Say the sounds, write did, met, bet

a. You're going to write the word (pause) **did.** Say the sounds in **did.** Get ready. (Signal for each sound as the children say) *d* (pause) *iii* (pause) *d.* (Repeat until firm.)
b. Everybody, write the word (pause) **did.** ✓
c. (Repeat *a* and *b* for **met, bet.**)

EXERCISE 5

Write is, has, that, ran, bad, me

a. You're going to write the word (pause) **is.** Think about the sounds in **is** and write the word. ✓
b. (Repeat *a* for **has, that, ran, bad, me.**)

SENTENCE WRITING

EXERCISE 6

Write one sentence

a. Listen to this sentence. **He has a cat.** Say that sentence. Get ready. (Signal.) *He has a cat.*
b. Now you're going to say that sentence the slow way. Get ready. (Signal for each word as the children say) *He* (pause) *has* (pause) *a* (pause) *cat.*

c. Everybody, write the sentence. Spell each word the right way. ✓

END OF SPELLING LESSON 106

Lesson 107

SOUND WRITING

EXERCISE 1

Reinforce sound combination sh

a. (Write on the board: **sh.**)
b. (Point to **sh.**) Everybody, tell me the sound these letters make. Get ready. (Signal.) *shshsh.* Yes, **shshsh.**
c. (Erase **sh.**) Everybody, write the letters that go together and make the sound **sh.** ✓

WORD WRITING

EXERCISE 2

Write sound combination words ship, she, wish, fish

a. (Write on the board: **ship, she, wish, fish.**)
b. (Point to **ship.**) Everybody, read this word the fast way. Get ready. (Signal.) *Ship.* Yes, **ship.**

c. Everybody, say the sounds you write for the word (pause) **ship.** Get ready. (Touch **sh, i, p** as the children say) *shshsh* (pause) *iii* (pause) *p.* (Repeat until firm.)

d. (Erase **ship.**) Everybody, write the word (pause) **ship.** ✓

e. (Repeat *b* through *d* for **she, wish, fish.**)

EXERCISE 3

Say the sounds, write **was, will**

a. You're going to write the word (pause) **was.** Say the sounds you write for (pause) **was.** Get ready. (Signal for each sound as the children say) *www* (pause) *aaa* (pause) *sss.* (Repeat until firm.)

b. Everybody, write the word (pause) **was.** ✓

c. (Repeat *a* and *b* for **will.**)

EXERCISE 4

Say the sounds, write **this, him, far**

a. You're going to write the word (pause) **this.** Say the sounds in **this.** Get ready. (Signal for each sound as the children say) *ththth* (pause) *iii* (pause) *sss.* (Repeat until firm.)

b. Everybody, write the word (pause) **this.** ✓

c. (Repeat *a* and *b* for **him, far.**)

EXERCISE 5

Write **did, hat, men, car**

a. You're going to write the word (pause) **did.** Think about the sounds in **did** and write the word. ✓

b. (Repeat *a* for **hat, men, car.**)

SENTENCE WRITING

EXERCISE 6

Write one sentence

a. Listen to this sentence. **He has a sad rat.** Say that sentence. Get ready. (Signal.) *He has a sad rat.*

b. Now you're going to say that sentence the slow way. Get ready. (Signal for each word as the children say) *He* (pause) *has* (pause) *a* (pause) *sad* (pause) *rat.*

c. Everybody, write the sentence. Spell each word the right way. ✓

END OF SPELLING LESSON 107

Lesson 108

SOUND WRITING

EXERCISE 1

Write **sh**

a. Everybody, you're going to write the letters that go together and make the sound **sh.** What sound? (Signal.) *shshsh.*

b. Write **sh.** ✓

WORD WRITING

EXERCISE 2

Write sound combination words **she, fish, ship, dish**

a. (Write on the board: **she, fish, ship, dish.**)

b. (Point to **she.**) Everybody, read this word the fast way. Get ready. (Signal.) *She.* Yes, **she.**

c. Everybody, say the sounds you write for the word (pause) **she.** Get ready. (Touch **sh, e** as the children say) *shshsh* (pause) *ēēē.* (Repeat until firm.)

d. (Erase **she.**) Everybody, write the word (pause) **she.** ✓

e. (Repeat *b* through *d* for **fish, ship, dish.**)

EXERCISE 3

Say the sounds, write **was, cop, top**

a. You're going to write the word (pause) **was.** Say the sounds in **was.** Get ready. (Signal for each sound as the children say) *www* (pause) *aaa* (pause) *sss.* (Repeat until firm.)

b. Everybody, write the word (pause) **was.** ✓

c. (Repeat *a* and *b* for **cop, top.**)

Write **not, hot, barn, arm, then**

a. You're going to write the word (pause) **not.** Think about the sounds in **not** and write the word. ✓
b. (Repeat *a* for **hot, barn, arm, then.**)

SENTENCE WRITING

Write one sentence

a. Listen to this sentence. **She has a ram.** Say that sentence. Get ready. (Signal.) *She has a ram.*
b. Now you're going to say that sentence the slow way. Get ready. (Signal for each word as the children say) *She* (pause) *has* (pause) *a* (pause) *ram.*
c. Everybody, write the sentence. Spell each word the right way. ✓

END OF SPELLING LESSON 108

Lesson 109

SOUND WRITING

Write **sh**

a. Everybody, you're going to write the letters that go together and make the sound **sh.** What sound? (Signal.) *shshsh.*
b. Write **sh.** ✓

WORD WRITING

Write sound combination words **dish, ship, shop**

a. (Write on the board: **dish, ship, shop.**)
b. (Point to **dish.**) Everybody, read this word the fast way. Get ready. (Signal.) *Dish.* Yes, **dish.**
c. Everybody, say the sounds you write for the word (pause) **dish.** Get ready. (Touch **d, i, sh** as the children say) *d* (pause) *iii* (pause) *sh.* (Repeat until firm.)
d. (Erase **dish.**) Everybody, write the word (pause) **dish.** ✓
e. (Repeat *b* through *d* for **ship, shop.**)

Write **car, was, has, is**

a. You're going to write the word (pause) **car.** Everybody think about the sounds in (pause) **car** and write the word. ✓
b. (Repeat *a* and *b* for **was, has, is.**)

Write **we, he, not, hop, far, did, this**

a. You're going to write the word (pause) **we.** Think about the sounds in **we** and write the word. ✓
b. (Repeat *a* for **he, not, hop, far, did, this.**)

SENTENCE WRITING

Write one sentence

a. Listen to this sentence. **That cop has fish.** Say that sentence. Get ready. (Signal.) *That cop has fish.*
b. Now you're going to say that sentence the slow way. Get ready. (Signal for each word as the children say) *That* (pause) *cop* (pause) *has* (pause) *fish.*
c. Everybody, write the sentence. Spell each word the right way. ✓

END OF SPELLING LESSON 109

Lesson 110

WORD WRITING

Say the sounds, write shop, barn, wet, dish, will

a. You're going to write the word (pause) **shop.** Say the sounds in **shop.** Get ready. (Signal for each sound as the children say) *shshsh* (pause) *ooo* (pause) *p.*
(Repeat until firm.)
b. Everybody, write the word (pause) **shop.** ✓
c. (Repeat *a* and *b* for **barn, wet, dish, will.**)

EXERCISE 2

Write ten, met, fat, was, is, that, hat, hop, cop

a. You're going to write the word (pause) **ten.** Think about the sounds in **ten** and write the word. ✓
b. (Repeat *a* for **met, fat, was, is, that, hat, hop, cop.**)

SENTENCE WRITING

EXERCISE 3

Write one sentence

a. Listen to this sentence. **She is not sad.** Say that sentence. Get ready. (Signal.) *She is not sad.*
b. Now you're going to say that sentence the slow way. Get ready. (Signal.) (Signal for each word as the children say) *She* (pause) *is* (pause) *not* (pause) *sad.*
c. Everybody, write the sentence. Spell each word the right way. ✓

END OF SPELLING LESSON 110

Lesson 111

WORD WRITING

EXERCISE 1

Listen, say the sounds, write his

a. You're going to write the word (pause) **his.** When you write the word **his,** you write these sounds: **h** (pause) **iii** (pause) **sss.**
b. Say the sounds you write for (pause) **his.** Get ready. (Signal for each sound as the children say) *h* (pause) *iii* (pause) *sss.*
(Repeat until firm.)
c. Everybody, write the word (pause) **his.** ✓

EXERCISE 2

Say the sounds, write ship, wish, farm, him, then

a. You're going to write the word (pause) **ship.** Say the sounds in **ship.** Get ready. (Signal for each sound as the children say) *shshsh* (pause) *iii* (pause) *p.*
(Repeat until firm.)
b. Everybody, write the word (pause) **ship.** ✓
c. (Repeat *a* and *b* for **wish, farm, him, then.**)

EXERCISE 3

Write bet, wet, that, arm, cop, hop, shop

a. You're going to write the word (pause) **bet.** Think about the sounds in **bet** and write the word. ✓
b. (Repeat *a* for **wet, that, arm, cop, hop, shop.**)

SENTENCE WRITING

EXERCISE 4

Write one sentence

a. Listen to this sentence. **She did not shop.** Say that sentence. Get ready. (Signal.) *She did not shop.*

b. Now you're going to say that sentence the slow way. Get ready. (Signal.) (Signal for each word as the children say) *She* (pause) *did* (pause) *not* (pause) *shop.*

c. Everybody, write the sentence. Spell each word the right way. ✓

END OF SPELLING LESSON 111

Lesson 112

WORD WRITING

Say the sounds, write **is, his, if, tar, them, set**

a. You're going to write the word (pause) **is.** Say the sounds in **is.** Get ready. (Signal for each sound as the children say) *iii* (pause) *sss.* (Repeat until firm.)

b. Everybody, write the word (pause) **is.** ✓

c. (Repeat *a* and *b* for **his, if, tar, them, set.**)

EXERCISE 2

Write **bar, was, hot, met, this**

a. You're going to write the word (pause) **bar.** Think about the sounds in **bar** and write the word. ✓

b. (Repeat *a* for **was, hot, met, this.**)

SENTENCE WRITING

EXERCISE 3

Write one sentence

a. Listen to this sentence. **We did not shop.** Say that sentence. Get ready. (Signal.) *We did not shop.*

b. Now you're going to say that sentence the slow way. Get ready. (Signal for each word as the children say) *We* (pause) *did* (pause) *not* (pause) *shop.*

c. Everybody, write the sentence. Spell each word the right way. ✓

END OF SPELLING LESSON 112

Lesson 113

SOUND WRITING

EXERCISE 1

Introduce sound combination **ing**

a. (Write on the board: **ing.**)

b. (Point to **ing.**) Everybody, tell me the sound these letters make. Get ready. (Signal.) *ing.* Yes, **ing.**

c. (Erase **ing.**) Everybody, write the letters that go together and make the sound **ing.** ✓

WORD WRITING

EXERCISE 2

Say the sounds, write **has, his, mop, mat, went, wish**

a. You're going to write the word (pause) **has.** Say the sounds in **has.** Get ready. (Signal for each sound as the children say) *h* (pause) *aaa* (pause) *sss.* (Repeat until firm.)

b. Everybody, write the word (pause) **has.** ✓

c. (Repeat *a* and *b* for **his, mop, mat, went, wish.**)

EXERCISE 3

Write **far, barn, we, it, then, bad**

a. You're going to write the word (pause) **far.** Think about the sounds in **far** and write the word. ✓

b. (Repeat *a* for **barn, we, it, then, bad.**)

SENTENCE WRITING

EXERCISE 4

Write one sentence

a. Listen to this sentence. **That dish was hot.** Say that sentence. Get ready. (Signal.) *That dish was hot.*

b. Now you're going to say that sentence the slow way. Get ready. (Signal for each word as the children say) *That* (pause) *dish* (pause) *was* (pause) *hot.*
c. Everybody, write the sentence. Spell each word the right way. ✓

END OF SPELLING LESSON 113

Lesson 114

SOUND WRITING

Reinforce sound combination ing

a. (Write on the board: **ing.**)
b. (Point to **ing.**) Everybody, tell me the sound these letters make. Get ready. (Signal.) *ing.* Yes, **ing.**
c. (Erase **ing.**) Everybody, write the letters that go together and make the sound **ing.** ✓

WORD WRITING

EXERCISE 2

Write sound combination words ring, sing, thing

a. (Write on the board: **ring, sing, thing.**)
b. (Point to **ring.**) Everybody, read this word the fast way. Get ready. (Signal.) *Ring.* Yes, **ring.**

c. Everybody, say the sounds you write for the word (pause) **ring.** Get ready. (Touch **r, ing** as the children say) *rrr* (pause) *ing.*
(Repeat until firm.)
d. (Erase **ring.**) Everybody, write the word (pause) **ring.** ✓
e. (Repeat *b* through *d* for **sing, thing.**)

EXERCISE 3

Say the sounds, write cow, how, now, went

a. (Write on the board: **cow, how, now, went.**)
b. (Point to **cow.**) Everybody, read this word the fast way. Get ready. (Signal.) *Cow.* Yes, **cow.**
c. Everybody, say the sounds you write for the word **cow.** Get ready. (Signal for each sound as the children say) *c* (pause) *ooo* (pause) *www.* (Repeat until firm.)
d. Everybody, write the word (pause) **cow.** ✓
e. (Repeat *a* and *b* for **how, now, went.**)

EXERCISE 4

Write car, farm, if, him, ship

a. You're going to write the word (pause) **car.** Think about the sounds in **car** and write the word. ✓
b. (Repeat *a* for **farm, if, him, ship.**)

SENTENCE WRITING

EXERCISE 5

Write one sentence

a. Listen to this sentence. **A fish was in a dish.** Say that sentence. Get ready. (Signal.) *A fish was in a dish.*
b. Now you're going to say that sentence the slow way. Get ready. (Signal for each word as the children say) *A* (pause) *fish* (pause) *was* (pause) *in* (pause) *a* (pause) *dish.*
c. Everybody, write the sentence. Spell each word the right way. ✓

END OF SPELLING LESSON 114

Lesson 115

SOUND WRITING

EXERCISE 1

Write ing

a. Everybody, you're going to write the letters that go together and make the sound **ing.** What sound? (Signal.) *ing.*
b. Write **ing.** ✓

WORD WRITING

Write sound combination words sing, thing, ring

a. (Write on the board: **sing, thing, ring.**)
b. (Point to **sing.**) Everybody, read this word the fast way. Get ready. (Signal.) *Sing.* Yes, **sing.**
c. Everybody, say the sounds you write for the word (pause) **sing.** Get ready. (Touch **s, ing** as the children say) *sss* (pause) *ing.*
(Repeat until firm.)
d. (Erase **sing.**) Everybody, write the word (pause) **sing.** ✓
e. (Repeat b through d for **thing, ring.**)

Listen, say the sounds, write on

a. You're going to write the word (pause) **on.** When you write the word **on,** you write these sounds: **ooo** (pause) **nnn.**
b. Say the sounds you write for (pause) **on.** Get ready. (Signal for each sound as the children say) *ooo* (pause) *nnn.* (Repeat until firm.)
c. Everybody, write the word (pause) **on.** ✓

Say the sounds, write hen, went, dug, bug, run, sun

a. You're going to write the word (pause) **hen.** Say the sounds in **hen.** Get ready. (Signal for each sound as the children say) *h* (pause) *eee* (pause) *nnn.*
(Repeat until firm.)
b. Everybody, write the word (pause) **hen.** ✓
c. (Repeat a and b for **went, dug, bug, run, sun.**)

Write how, will, has

a. You're going to write the word (pause) **how.** Think about the sounds in **how** and write the word. ✓
b. (Repeat a for **will, has.**)

SENTENCE WRITING

Write one sentence

a. Listen to this sentence. **The cow was in the barn.** Say that sentence. Get ready. (Signal.) *The cow was in the barn.*
b. Now you're going to say that sentence the slow way. Get ready. (Signal for each word as the children say) *The* (pause) *cow* (pause) *was* (pause) *in* (pause) *the* (pause) *barn.*
c. Everybody, write the sentence. Spell each word the right way. ✓

END OF SPELLING LESSON 115

Lesson 116

WORD WRITING

Say the sounds, write thing, shop, park

a. You're going to write the word (pause) **thing.** Say the sounds in **thing.** Get ready. (Signal for each sound as the children say) *ththth* (pause) *ing.*
(Repeat until firm.)
b. Everybody, write the word (pause) **thing.** ✓
c. (Repeat a and b for **shop, park.**)

Write cop, wish, far, ring, rug, fun, bug, now, how

a. You're going to write the word (pause) **cop.** Think about the sounds in **cop** and write the word. ✓

b. (Repeat *a* for **wish, far, ring, rug, fun, bug, now, how.**)

SENTENCE WRITING

EXERCISE 3

Write one sentence

a. Listen to this sentence. **The hen was on a farm.** Say that sentence. Get ready. (Signal.) *The hen was on a farm.*

b. Now you're going to say that sentence the slow way. Get ready. (Signal for each word as the children say) *The* (pause) *hen* (pause) *was* (pause) *on* (pause) *a* (pause) *farm.*

c. Everybody, write the sentence. Spell each word the right way. ✓

END OF SPELLING LESSON 116

Lesson 117

WORD WRITING

EXERCISE 1

Listen, say the sounds, write to, do

a. You're going to write the word (pause) **to.** When you write the word **to,** you write these sounds: **t** (pause) **ooo.**

b. Say the sounds you write for (pause) **to.** Get ready. (Signal for each sound as the children say) *t* (pause) *ooo.* (Repeat until firm.)

c. Everybody, write the word (pause) **to.** ✓

d. (Repeat *a* through *c* for **do.**)

EXERCISE 2

Say the sounds, write if, cow, dark, sing, park

a. You're going to write the word (pause) **if.** Say the sounds in **if.** Get ready. (Signal for each sound as the children say) *iii* (pause) *fff.* (Repeat until firm.)

b. Everybody, write the word (pause) **if.** ✓

c. (Repeat *a* and *b* for **cow, dark, sing, park.**)

EXERCISE 3

Write on, hen, then, now, dug, run, sun

a. You're going to write the word (pause) **on.** Think about the sounds in **on** and write the word. ✓

b. (Repeat *a* for **hen, then, now, dug, run, sun.**)

SENTENCE WRITING

EXERCISE 4

Write one sentence

a. Listen to this sentence. **She was in the park.** Say that sentence. Get ready. (Signal.) *She was in the park.*

b. Now you're going to say that sentence the slow way. Get ready. (Signal for each word as the children say) *She* (pause) *was* (pause) *in* (pause) *the* (pause) *park.*

c. Everybody, write the sentence. Spell each word the right way. ✓

END OF SPELLING LESSON 117

Lesson 118

WORD WRITING

EXERCISE 1

Say the sounds, write to, do, bag, and, dig, ship, shop

a. You're going to write the word (pause) **to.** Say the sounds in **to.** Get ready. (Signal for each sound as the children say) *t* (pause) *ooo.* (Repeat until firm.)

b. Everybody, write the word (pause) **to.** ✓

c. (Repeat *a* and *b* for **do, bag, and, dig, ship, shop.**)

Write **far, thing, has, how**

a. You're going to write the word (pause) **far.** Think about the sounds in **far** and write the word. ✓

b. (Repeat *a* for **thing, has, how.**)

SENTENCE WRITING

Write two sentences

a. Listen to this sentence. **The park was not dark.** Say that sentence. Get ready. (Signal.) *The park was not dark.*

b. Now you're going to say that sentence the slow way. Get ready. (Signal for each word as the children say) *The* (pause) *park* (pause) *was* (pause) *not* (pause) *dark.*

c. Everybody, write the sentence. Spell each word the right way. ✓

d. (Repeat *a* through *c* for **He has a cat.**)

END OF SPELLING LESSON 118

Lesson 119

WORD WRITING

Say the sounds, write **ring, dog, met, him, bark**

a. You're going to write the word (pause) **ring.** Say the sounds in **ring.** Get ready. (Clap for each sound as the children say) *rrr* (pause) *ing.* (Repeat until firm.)

b. Everybody, write the word (pause) **ring.** ✓

c. (Repeat *a* and *b* for **dog, met, him, bark.**)

Write **went, that, bug, cop, has, big, how**

a. You're going to write the word (pause) **went.** Think about the sounds in **went** and write the word. ✓

b. (Repeat *a* for **that, bug, cop, has, big, how.**)

SENTENCE WRITING

Write two sentences

a. Listen to this sentence. **His fish was not fat.** Say that sentence. Get ready. (Signal.) *His fish was not fat.*

b. Now you're going to say that sentence the slow way. Get ready. (Signal for each word as the children say) *His* (pause) *fish* (pause) *was* (pause) *not* (pause) *fat.*

c. Everybody, write the sentence. Spell each word the right way. ✓

d. (Repeat *a* through *c* for **She is fat and sad.**)

END OF SPELLING LESSON 119

Lesson 120

WORD WRITING

Say the sounds, write **can, if, do, us, get, set**

a. You're going to write the word (pause) **can.** Say the sounds in **can.** Get ready. (Signal for each sound as the children say) *c* (pause) *aaa* (pause) *nnn.* (Repeat until firm.)

b. Everybody, write the word (pause) **can.** ✓

c. (Repeat *a* and *b* for **if, do, us, get, set.**)

Write **to, has, sing, far, rug, ship, shop**

a. You're going to write the word (pause) **to.** Think about the sounds in **to** and write the word. ✓

b. (Repeat *a* for **has, sing, far, rug, ship, shop.**)

SENTENCE WRITING

Write two sentences

a. Listen to this sentence. **His hat is not wet.** Say that sentence. Get ready. (Signal.) *His hat is not wet.*

b. Now you're going to say that sentence the slow way. Get ready. (Signal for each word as the children say) *His* (pause) *hat* (pause) *is* (pause) *not* (pause) *wet.*

c. Everybody, write the sentence. Spell each word the right way. ✓

d. (Repeat *a* through *c* for **We will run and hop.**)

END OF SPELLING LESSON 120

Lesson 121

WORD WRITING

Listen, say the sounds, write **come**

a. You're going to write the word (pause) **come.** When you write the word **come,** you write these sounds: **c** (pause) **ooo** (pause) **mmm** (pause) **ēēē.**

b. Say the sounds you write for (pause) **come.** Get ready. (Signal for each sound as the children say) *c* (pause) *ooo* (pause) *mmm* (pause) *ēēē.* (Repeat until firm.)

c. Everybody, write the word (pause) **come.** ✓

Say the sounds, write **bag, bug, thing, with**

a. You're going to write the word (pause) **bag.** Say the sounds in **bag.** Get ready. (Signal for each sound as the children say) *b* (pause) *aaa* (pause) *g.* (Repeat until firm.)

b. Everybody, write the word (pause) **bag.** ✓

c. (Repeat *a* and *b* for **bug, thing, with.**)

Write **sing, do, us, car, get, in**

a. You're going to write the word (pause) **sing.** Think about the sounds in **sing** and write the word. ✓

b. (Repeat *a* for **do, us, car, get, in.**)

SENTENCE WRITING

Write two sentences

a. Listen to this sentence. **He has a cat and a rat.** Say that sentence. Get ready. (Signal.) *He has a cat and a rat.*

b. Now you're going to say that sentence the slow way. Get ready. (Signal for each word as the children say) *He* (pause) *has* (pause) *a* (pause) *cat* (pause) *and* (pause) *a* (pause) *rat.*

c. Everybody, write the sentence. Spell each word the right way. ✓

d. (Repeat *a* through *c* for **The cop was in the park.**)

END OF SPELLING LESSON 121

Lesson 122

WORD WRITING

EXERCISE 1

Listen, say the sounds, write come

a. You're going to write the word (pause) **come.** When you write the word **come,** you write these sounds: **c** (pause) **ooo** (pause) **mmm** (pause) **ēēē.**

b. Say the sounds you write for (pause) **come.** Get ready. (Signal for each sound as the children say) *c* (pause) *ooo* (pause) *mmm* (pause) *ēēē.* (Repeat until firm.)

c. Everybody, write the word (pause) **come.** ✓

EXERCISE 2

Say the sounds, write how, cow, with

a. You're going to write the word (pause) **how.** Say the sounds in **how.** Get ready. (Signal for each sound as the children say) *h* (pause) *ooo* (pause) *www.* (Repeat until firm.)

b. Everybody, write the word (pause) **how.** ✓

c. (Repeat *a* and *b* for **cow, with.**)

EXERCISE 3

Listen, say the sounds, write pill, hill

a. You're going to write the word (pause) **pill.** When you write the word **pill,** you write these sounds: **p** (pause) **iii** (pause) **lll** (pause) **lll.**

b. Say the sounds you write for (pause) **pill.** Get ready. (Signal for each sound as the children say) *p* (pause) *iii* (pause) *lll* (pause) *lll.* (Repeat until firm.)

c. Everybody, write the word (pause) **pill.** ✓

d. (Repeat *a* through *c* for **hill.**)

EXERCISE 4

Write wish, barn, red, to, ring, has

a. You're going to write the word (pause) **wish.** Think about the sounds in **wish** and write the word. ✓

b. (Repeat *a* for **barn, red, to, ring, has.**)

SENTENCE WRITING

EXERCISE 5

Write two sentences

a. Listen to this sentence. **She will hop and sing.** Say that sentence. Get ready. (Signal.) *She will hop and sing.*

b. Now you're going to say that sentence the slow way. Get ready. (Signal for each word as the children say) *She* (pause) *will* (pause) *hop* (pause) *and* (pause) *sing.*

c. Everybody, write the sentence. Spell each word the right way. ✓

d. (Repeat *a* through *c* for **A bug was on a rug.**)

END OF SPELLING LESSON 122

Lesson 123

WORD WRITING

EXERCISE 1

Say the sounds, write cup, us, come, swim, bed, get

a. You're going to write the word (pause) **cup.** Say the sounds in **cup.** Get ready. (Signal for each sound as the children say) *c* (pause) *uuu* (pause) *p.* (Repeat until firm.)

b. Everybody, write the word (pause) **cup.** ✓

c. (Repeat *a* and *b* for **us, come, swim, bed, get.**)

Write dish, with, hill, arm

a. You're going to write the word (pause) **dish.** Think about the sounds in **dish** and write the word. ✓

b. (Repeat *a* for **with, hill, arm.**)

SENTENCE WRITING

EXERCISE 3

Write two sentences

a. Listen to this sentence. **The cat was in the car.** Say that sentence. Get ready. (Signal.) *The cat was in the car.*

b. Now you're going to say that sentence the slow way. Get ready. (Signal for each word as the children say) *The* (pause) *cat* (pause) *was* (pause) *in* (pause) *the* (pause) *car.*

c. Everybody, write the sentence. Spell each word the right way. ✓

d. (Repeat *a* through *c* for **That fan is not wet.**)

END OF SPELLING LESSON 123

Lesson 124

WORD WRITING

EXERCISE 1

Say the sounds, write us, bus, top, stop, fed

a. You're going to write the word (pause) **us.** Say the sounds in **us.** Get ready. (Signal for each sound as the children say) *uuu* (pause) *sss.* (Repeat until firm.)

b. Everybody, write the word (pause) **us.** ✓

c. (Repeat *a* and *b* for **bus, top, stop, fed.**)

EXERCISE 2

Write bed, swim, if, come, wish, me, has

a. You're going to write the word (pause) **bed.** Think about the sounds in **bed** and write the word. ✓

b. (Repeat *a* for **swim, if, come, wish, me, has.**)

SENTENCE WRITING

EXERCISE 3

Write two sentences

a. Listen to this sentence. **The rat was on the ship.** Say that sentence. Get ready. (Signal.) *The rat was on the ship.*

b. Now you're going to say that sentence the slow way. Get ready. (Signal for each word as the children say) *The* (pause) *rat* (pause) *was* (pause) *on* (pause) *the* (pause) *ship.*

c. Everybody, write the sentence. Spell each word the right way. ✓

d. (Repeat *a* through *c* for **A dog will run and bark.**)

END OF SPELLING LESSON 124

Lesson 125

WORD WRITING

EXERCISE 1

Say the sounds, write big, pit, ring, sing, dark

a. You're going to write the word (pause) **big.** Say the sounds in **big.** Get ready. (Signal for each sound as the children say) *b* (pause) *iii* (pause) *g.* (Repeat until firm.)

b. Everybody, write the word (pause) **big.** ✓

c. (Repeat *a* and *b* for **pit, ring, sing, dark.**)

EXERCISE 2

Write **mop, cop, us, fed, them**

a. You're going to write the word (pause) **mop.** Think about the sounds in **mop** and write the word. ✓

b. (Repeat a for **cop, us, fed, them.**)

SENTENCE WRITING

EXERCISE 3

Write two sentences

a. Listen to this sentence. **This fish will swim.** Say that sentence. Get ready. (Signal.) *This fish will swim.*

b. Now you're going to say that sentence the slow way. Get ready. (Signal for each word as the children say) *This* (pause) *fish* (pause) *will* (pause) *swim.*

c. Everybody, write the sentence. Spell each word the right way. ✓

d. (Repeat a through c for **She did not hit me.**)

END OF SPELLING LESSON 125

Lesson 126

WORD WRITING

EXERCISE 1

Listen, say the sounds, write **said**

a. You're going to write the word (pause) **said.** When you write the word **said,** you write these sounds: **sss** (pause) **aaa** (pause) **iii** (pause) **d.**

b. Say the sounds you write for (pause) **said.** Get ready. (Signal for each sound as the children say) *sss* (pause) *aaa* (pause) *iii* (pause) *d.* (Repeat until firm.)

c. Everybody, write the word (pause) **said.** ✓

EXERCISE 2

Say the sounds, write **come, him, then, went, to**

a. You're going to write the word (pause) **come.** Say the sounds in **come.** Get ready. (Signal for each sound as the children say) *c* (pause) *ooo* (pause) *mmm* (pause) *ēēē.* (Repeat until firm.)

b. Everybody, write the word (pause) **come.** ✓

c. (Repeat a and b for **him, then, went, to.**)

EXERCISE 3

Write **has, thing, with, get, us, hop**

a. You're going to write the word (pause) **has.** Think about the sounds in **has** and write the word. ✓

b. (Repeat a for **thing, with, get, us, hop.**)

SENTENCE WRITING

EXERCISE 4

Write two sentences

a. Listen to this sentence. **That man did not run.** Say that sentence. Get ready. (Signal.) *That man did not run.*

b. Now you're going to say that sentence the slow way. Get ready. (Signal for each word as the children say) *That* (pause) *man* (pause) *did* (pause) *not* (pause) *run.*

c. Everybody, write the sentence. Spell each word the right way. ✓

d. (Repeat a through c for **This park is not big.**)

END OF SPELLING LESSON 126

Lesson 127

WORD WRITING

EXERCISE 1

Listen, say the sounds, write said

a. You're going to write the word (pause) **said.** When you write the word **said,** you write these sounds: **sss** (pause) **aaa** (pause) **iii** (pause) **d.**

b. Say the sounds you write for (pause) **said.** Get ready. (Signal for each sound as the children say) *sss* (pause) *aaa* (pause) *iii* (pause) *d.* (Repeat until firm.)

c. Everybody, write the word (pause) **said.** ✓

EXERCISE 2

Say the sounds, write come, tar, if

a. You're going to write the word (pause) **come.** Say the sounds in **come.** Get ready. (Signal for each sound as the children say) *c* (pause) *ooo* (pause) *mmm* (pause) *ēēē.* (Repeat until firm.)

b. Everybody, write the word (pause) **come.** ✓

c. (Repeat *a* and *b* for **tar, if.**)

EXERCISE 3

Write us, bus, with, hill, ring

a. You're going to write the word (pause) **us.** Think about the sounds in **us** and write the word. ✓

b. (Repeat *a* for **bus, with, hill, ring.**)

SENTENCE WRITING

EXERCISE 4

Write two sentences

a. Listen to this sentence. **That cow did not sing.** Say that sentence. Get ready. (Signal.) *That cow did not sing.*

b. Now you're going to say that sentence the slow way. Get ready. (Signal for each word as the children say) *That* (pause) *cow* (pause) *did* (pause) *not* (pause) *sing.*

c. Everybody, write the sentence. Spell each word the right way. ✓

d. (Repeat *a* through *c* for **This bug will run and hop.**)

END OF SPELLING LESSON 127

Lesson 128

WORD WRITING

EXERCISE 1

Say the sounds, write sell, tell, bell, well

a. (Write on the board: **sell, tell, bell, well.**)

b. (Point to **sell.**) Everybody, read this word the fast way. Get ready. (Signal.) *Sell.* Yes, **sell.**

c. Everybody, say the sounds you write in the word in **sell.** Get ready. (Signal for each sound as the children say) *sss* (pause) *eee* (pause) *lll* (pause) *lll.* (Repeat until firm.)

d. Everybody, write the word (pause) **sell.** ✓

e. Repeat *a* and *b* for **tell, bell, well.**

EXERCISE 2

Write bet, ten, bug, mud, now, hit, swim

a. You're going to write the word (pause) **bet.** Think about the sounds in **bet** and write the word. ✓

b. (Repeat *a* for **ten, bug, mud, now, hit, swim.**)

SENTENCE WRITING

Write two sentences

a. Listen to this sentence. **We went to the farm.** Say that sentence. Get ready. (Signal.) *We went to the farm.*

b. Now you're going to say that sentence the slow way. Get ready. (Signal for each word as the children say) *We* (pause) *went* (pause) *to* (pause) *the* (pause) *farm.*

c. Everybody, write the sentence. Spell each word the right way. ✓

d. (Repeat *a* through *c* for **She will come with me.**)

END OF SPELLING LESSON 128

Lesson 129

WORD WRITING

EXERCISE 1

Say the sounds, write **bell, fell, sell, thing, me, she**

a. You're going to write the word (pause) **bell.** Say the sounds in **bell.** Get ready. (Signal for each sound as the children say) *b* (pause) *eee* (pause) *lll* (pause) *lll.*
(Repeat until firm.)

b. Everybody, write the word (pause) **bell.** ✓

c. (Repeat *a* and *b* for **fell, sell, thing, me, she.**)

EXERCISE 2

Write **do, said, them, come, hill, mad**

a. You're going to write the word (pause) **do.** Think about the sounds in **do** and write the word. ✓

b. (Repeat *a* for **said, them, come, hill, mad.**)

SENTENCE WRITING

EXERCISE 3

Write two sentences

a. Listen to this sentence. **The dog went to the barn.** Say that sentence. Get ready. (Signal.) *The dog went to the barn.*

b. Now you're going to say that sentence the slow way. Get ready. (Signal for each word as the children say) *The* (pause) *dog* (pause) *went* (pause) *to* (pause) *the* (pause) *barn.*

c. Everybody, write the sentence. Spell each word the right way. ✓

d. (Repeat *a* through *c* for **A cow will run with us.**)

END OF SPELLING LESSON 129

Lesson 130

WORD WRITING

EXERCISE 1

Say the sounds, write **dish, wish, fish, if, bark, sand**

a. You're going to write the word (pause) **dish.** Say the sounds in **dish.** Get ready. (Signal for each sound as the children say) *d* (pause) *iii* (pause) *sh.* (Repeat until firm.)

b. Everybody, write the word (pause) **dish.** ✓

c. (Repeat *a* and *b* for **wish, fish, if, bark, sand.**)

EXERCISE 2

Write **well, tell, said, his, has**

a. You're going to write the word (pause) **well.** Think about the sounds in **well** and write the word. ✓

b. (Repeat *a* for **tell, said, his, has.**)

SENTENCE WRITING

EXERCISE 3

Write two sentences

a. Listen to this sentence. **He will come with us.** Say that sentence. Get ready. (Signal.) *He will come with us.*

b. Now you're going to say that sentence the slow way. Get ready. (Signal for each word as the children say) *He* (pause) *will* (pause) *come* (pause) *with* (pause) *us.*

c. Everybody, write the sentence. Spell each word the right way. ✓

d. (Repeat *a* through *c* for **That cop was mad.**)

END OF SPELLING LESSON 130

Lesson 131

WORD WRITING

Say the sounds, write **cup, up, us, bell, ship, cow**

a. You're going to write the word **cup.** Say the sounds in **cup.** Get ready. (Signal for each sound as the children say) *c* (pause) *uuu* (pause) *p.* (Repeat until firm.)

b. Everybody, write the word (pause) **cup.** ✓

c. (Repeat *a* and *b* for **up, us, bell, ship, cow.**)

Write **to, went, car, fell, sing, how**

a. You're going to write the word (pause) **to.** Think about the sounds in **to** and write the word. ✓

b. (Repeat *a* for **went, car, fell, sing, how.**)

SENTENCE WRITING

Write two sentences

a. Listen to this sentence. **That dish was in the mud.** Say that sentence. Get ready. (Signal.) *That dish was in the mud.*

b. Now you're going to say that sentence the slow way. Get ready. (Signal for each word as the children say) *That* (pause) *dish* (pause) *was* (pause) *in* (pause) *the* (pause) *mud.*

c. Everybody, write the sentence. Spell each word the right way. ✓

d. (Repeat *a* through *c* for **His dog will bark.**)

END OF SPELLING LESSON 131

Lesson 132

SOUND WRITING

Introduce sound combination al

a. (Write on the board: **al.**)

b. (Point to **al.**) Everybody, tell me the sound these letters make. Get ready. (Signal.) *All.* Yes, **all.**

c. (Erase **al.**) Everybody, write the two letters that go together and make the sound **all.** ✓

WORD WRITING

Say the sounds, write **swim, ring, wet, hand**

a. You're going to write the word (pause) **swim.** Say the sounds in **swim.** Get ready. (Signal for each sound as the children say) *sss* (pause) *www* (pause) *iii* (pause) *mmm.* (Repeat until firm.)

b. Everybody, write the word (pause) **swim.** ✓

c. (Repeat *a* and *b* for **ring, wet, hand.**)

EXERCISE 3

Write **sand, it, hill, well, met, said**

a. You're going to write the word (pause) **sand.** Think about the sounds in **sand** and write the word. ✓

b. (Repeat *a* for **it, hill, well, met, said.**)

SENTENCE WRITING

EXERCISE 4

Write two sentences

a. Listen to this sentence. **The hen sat on the fan.** Say that sentence. Get ready. (Signal.) *The hen sat on the fan.*

b. Now you're going to say that sentence the slow way. Get ready. (Signal for each word as the children say) *The* (pause) *hen* (pause) *sat* (pause) *on* (pause) *the* (pause) *fan.*

c. Everybody, write the sentence. Spell each word the right way. ✓

d. (Repeat *a* through *c* for **His cat ran in the park.**)

END OF SPELLING LESSON 132

SOUND WRITING

EXERCISE 1

Reinforce sound combination **al**

a. (Write on the board: **al.**)

b. (Point to **al.**) Everybody, tell me the sound these letters make. Get ready. (Signal.) *All.* Yes, **all.**

c. (Erase **al.**) Everybody, write the two letters that go together and make the sound **all.** ✓

WORD WRITING

EXERCISE 2

Write sound combination words **all, ball, fall, also**

a. (Write on the board: **all, ball, fall, also.**)

b. (Point to **all.**) Everybody, read this word the fast way. Get ready. (Signal.) *All.* Yes, **all.**

c. Everybody, say the sounds you write for the word (pause) **all.** Get ready. (Touch **al, l** as the children say) *al* (pause) *lll.*
(Repeat until firm.)

d. (Erase **all.**) Everybody, write the word (pause) **all.** ✓

e. (Repeat *b* through *d* for **ball, fall,** and **also.**)

EXERCISE 3

Say the sounds, write **cap, pig, nut**

a. You're going to write the word (pause) **cap.** Say the sounds in **cap.** Get ready. (Signal for each sound as the children say) *c* (pause) *aaa* (pause) *p.* (Repeat until firm.)

b. Everybody, write the word (pause) **cap.** ✓

c. (Repeat *a* and *b* for **pig, nut.**)

EXERCISE 4

Write **big, rug, bus, dark**

a. You're going to write the word (pause) **big.** Think about the sounds in **big** and write the word. ✓

b. (Repeat *a* for **rug, bus, dark.**)

SENTENCE WRITING

EXERCISE 5

Write two sentences

a. Listen to this sentence. **His dog can swim.** Say that sentence. Get ready. (Signal.) *His dog can swim.*

b. Now you're going to say that sentence the slow way. Get ready. (Signal for each word as the children say) *His* (pause) *dog* (pause) *can* (pause) *swim.*

c. Everybody, write the sentence. Spell each word the right way. ✓
d. (Repeat *a* through *c* for **She will sell a hat.**)

END OF SPELLING LESSON 133

Lesson 134

SOUND WRITING

Reinforce sound combination al

a. (Write on the board: **al.**)
b. (Point to **al.**) Everybody, tell me the sound these letters make. Get ready. (Signal.) *All.* Yes, **all.**
c. (Erase **al.**) Everybody, write the two letters that go together and make the sound **all.** ✓

WORD WRITING

Write sound combination words salt, call, fall

a. (Write on the board: **salt, call, fall.**)
b. (Point to **salt.**) Everybody, read this word the fast way. Get ready. (Signal.) *Salt.* Yes, **salt.**

c. Everybody, say the sounds you write for the word (pause) **salt.** Get ready. (Touch **s, al, t** as the children say) *sss* (pause) *al* (pause) *t.* (Repeat until firm.)
d. Erase **salt.** Everybody, write the word (pause) **salt.** ✓
e. (Repeat *b* through *d* for **call, fall.**)

Say the sounds, write come, bark

a. You're going to write the word (pause) **come.** Say the sounds in **come.** Get ready. (Signal for each sound as the children say) *c* (pause) *ooo* (pause) *mmm* (pause) *ēēē.* (Repeat until firm.)
b. Everybody, write the word (pause) **come.** ✓
c. (Repeat *a* and *b* for **bark.**)

Write sand, hand, bet, said, has, bug

a. You're going to write the word (pause) **sand.** Think about the sounds in **sand** and write the word. ✓
b. (Repeat *a* for **hand, bet, said, has, bug.**)

SENTENCE WRITING

Write two sentences

a. Listen to this sentence. **His pig went with him.** Say that sentence. Get ready. (Signal.) *His pig went with him.*
b. Now you're going to say that sentence the slow way. Get ready. (Signal for each word as the children say) *His* (pause) *pig* (pause) *went* (pause) *with* (pause) *him.*
c. Everybody, write the sentence. Spell each word the right way. ✓
d. (Repeat *a* through *c* for **His cap is in the mud.**)

END OF SPELLING LESSON 134

Lesson 135

WORD WRITING

Write sound combination words also, call, ball

a. (Write on the board: **also, call, ball.**)
b. (Point to **also.**) Everybody, read this word the fast way. Get ready. (Signal.) *Also.* Yes, **also.**

c. Everybody, say the sounds you write for the word (pause) **also.** Get ready. (Touch **al, s, o** as the children say) *al* (pause) *sss* (pause) *ōōō.* (Repeat until firm.)

d. (Erase **also.**) Everybody, write the word (pause) **also.** ✓

e. (Repeat *b* through *d* for **call, ball.**)

Say the sounds, write **how, wish, it, hit, shop, met, hand**

a. You're going to write the word (pause) **how.** Say the sounds in **how.** Get ready. (Signal for each sound as the children say) *h* (pause) *ooo* (pause) *www.* (Repeat until firm.)

b. Everybody, write the word (pause) **how.** ✓

c. (Repeat *a* and *b* for **wish, it, hit, shop, met, hand.**)

Write **do, if**

a. You're going to write the word (pause) **do.** Think about the sounds in **do** and write the word. ✓

b. (Repeat *a* for **if.**)

SENTENCE WRITING

Write two sentences

a. Listen to this sentence. **She will sell a bell.** Say that sentence. Get ready. (Signal.) *She will sell a bell.*

b. Now you're going to say that sentence the slow way. Get ready. (Signal for each word as the children say) *She* (pause) *will* (pause) *sell* (pause) *a* (pause) *bell.*

c. Everybody, write the sentence. Spell each word the right way. ✓

d. (Repeat *a* through *c* for **The nut was not fat.**)

END OF SPELLING LESSON 135.

Lesson 136

WORD WRITING

Write sound combination words **tall, salt, wall**

a. (Write on the board: **tall, salt, wall.**)

b. (Point to **tall.**) Everybody, read this word the fast way. Get ready. (Signal.) *Tall.* Yes, **tall.**

c. Everybody, say the sounds you write for the word (pause) **tall.** Get ready. (Touch **t, al, l** as the children say) *t* (pause) *al* (pause) *lll.* (Repeat until firm.)

d. (Erase **tall.**) Everybody, write the word (pause) **tall.** ✓

e. (Repeat *b* through *d* for **salt, wall.**)

Say the sounds, write **fell, card, rug**

a. You're going to write the word (pause) **fell.** Say the sounds in **fell.** Get ready. (Signal for each sound as the children say) *fff* (pause) *eee* (pause) *lll* (pause) *lll.* (Repeat until firm.)

b. Everybody, write the word (pause) **fell.** ✓

c. (Repeat *a* and *b* for **card, rug.**)

Write **did, big, cap, his, now**

a. You're going to write the word (pause) **did.** Think about the sounds in **did** and write the word. ✓

b. (Repeat *a* for **big, cap, his, now.**)

SENTENCE WRITING

EXERCISE 4

Write two sentences

a. Listen to this sentence. **The dog will sing with us.** Say that sentence. Get ready. (Signal.) *The dog will sing with us.*

b. Now you're going to say that sentence the slow way. Get ready. (Signal for each word as the children say) *The* (pause) *dog* (pause) *will* (pause) *sing* (pause) *with* (pause) *us.*

c. Everybody, write the sentence. Spell each word the right way. ✓

d. (Repeat *a* through *c* for **She is on the bus.**)

END OF SPELLING LESSON 136

Lesson 137

WORD WRITING

EXERCISE 1

Say the sounds, write tall, wall, wish, said, tap

a. You're going to write the word (pause) **tall.** Say the sounds in **tall.** Get ready. (Signal for each sound as the children say) *t* (pause) *al* (pause) *lll.* (Repeat until firm.)

b. Everybody, write the word (pause) **tall.** ✓

c. (Repeat *a* and *b* for **wall, wish, said, tap.**)

EXERCISE 2

Write them, tell, card, to, ship, cap

a. You're going to write the word (pause) **them.** Think about the sounds in **them** and write the word. ✓

b. (Repeat *a* for **tell, card, to, ship, cap.**)

SENTENCE WRITING

EXERCISE 3

Write two sentences

a. Listen to this sentence. **We will hop and sing.** Say that sentence. Get ready. (Signal.) *We will hop and sing.*

b. Now you're going to say that sentence the slow way. Get ready. (Signal for each word as the children say) *We* (pause) *will* (pause) *hop* (pause) *and* (pause) *sing.*

c. Everybody, write the sentence. Spell each word the right way. ✓

d. (Repeat *a* through *c* for **She did not hit me.**)

END OF SPELLING LESSON 137

Lesson 138

WORD WRITING

EXERCISE 1

Say the sounds, write salt, card, now, swim, this

a. You're going to write the word (pause) **salt.** Say the sounds in **salt.** Get ready. (Signal for each sound as the children say) *sss* (pause) *al* (pause) *t.* Repeat until firm.

b. Everybody, write the word (pause) **salt.** ✓

c. (Repeat *a* and *b* for **card, now, swim, this.**)

EXERCISE 2

Write call, fun, get, ring, ham

a. You're going to write the word (pause) **call.** Think about the sounds in **call** and write the word. ✓

b. (Repeat *a* for **fun, get, ring, ham.**)

SENTENCE WRITING

EXERCISE 3

Write two sentences

a. Listen to this sentence. **That bell did not ring.** Say that sentence. Get ready. (Signal.) *That bell did not ring.*

b. Now you're going to say that sentence the slow way. Get ready. (Signal for each word as the children say) *That* (pause) *bell* (pause) *did* (pause) *not* (pause) *ring.*

c. Everybody, write the sentence. Spell each word the right way. ✓

d. (Repeat *a* through *c* for **He can run with us.**)

END OF SPELLING LESSON 138

Lesson 139

WORD WRITING

EXERCISE 1

Listen, say the sounds, write of, stop

a. You're going to write the word (pause) **of.** When you write the word **of,** you write these sounds: **ooo** (pause) **fff.**

b. Say the sounds you write for (pause) **of.** Get ready. (Signal for each sound as the children say) *ooo* (pause) *fff.* (Repeat until firm.)

c. Everybody, write the word (pause) **of.** ✓

d. (Repeat *a* through *c* for **stop.**)

EXERCISE 2

Say the sounds, write to, also, went

a. You're going to write the word (pause) **to.** Say the sounds in **to.** Get ready. (Signal for each sound as the children say) *t* (pause) *ooo.* (Repeat until firm.)

b. Everybody, write the word (pause) **to.** ✓

c. (Repeat *a* and *b* for **also, went.**)

EXERCISE 3

Write fish, him, wall, hand, thing

a. You're going to write the word (pause) **fish.** Think about the sounds in **fish** and write the word. ✓

b. (Repeat *a* for **him, wall, hand, thing.**)

SENTENCE WRITING

EXERCISE 4

Write two sentences

a. Listen to this sentence. **His card is red.** Say that sentence. Get ready. (Signal.) *His card is red.*

b. Now you're going to say that sentence the slow way. Get ready. (Signal for each word as the children say) *His* (pause) *card* (pause) *is* (pause) *red.*

c. Everybody, write the sentence. Spell each word the right way. ✓

d. (Repeat *a* through *c* for **This cat has a bell.**)

END OF SPELLING LESSON 139

Lesson 140

WORD WRITING

EXERCISE 1

Say the sounds, write said, cup, of, stop

a. You're going to write the word (pause) **said.** Say the sounds in **said.** Get ready. (Signal for each sound as the children say) *sss* (pause) *aaa* (pause) *iii* (pause) *d.* (Repeat until firm.)

b. Everybody, write the word (pause) **said.** ✓

c. (Repeat *a* and *b* for **cup, of, stop.**)

EXERCISE 2

Write shop, if, big, fall, wet, met, us

a. You're going to write the word (pause) **shop.** Think about the sounds in **shop** and write the word. ✓

b. (Repeat *a* for **if, big, fall, wet, met, us.**)

SENTENCE WRITING

EXERCISE 3

Write two sentences

a. Listen to this sentence. **We will sit and sing.** Say that sentence. Get ready. (Signal.) *We will sit and sing.*

b. Now you're going to say that sentence the slow way. Get ready. (Signal for each word as the children say) *We* (pause) *will* (pause) *sit* (pause) *and* (pause) *sing.*

c. Everybody, write the sentence. Spell each word the right way. ✓

d. (Repeat a through c for **That cow did not bark.**)

END OF SPELLING LESSON 140

Lesson 141

SOUND WRITING

EXERCISE 1

Introduce sound combination wh

a. (Write on the board: **wh.**)

b. (Point to **wh.**) Everybody, tell me the sound these letters make. Get ready. (Signal.) *whwhwh.* Yes, **whwhwh.**

---

c. (Erase **wh.**) Everybody, write the letters that go together and make the sound **wh.** ✓

WORD WRITING

EXERCISE 2

Say the sounds, write sing, sand, arm, salt, swim

a. You're going to write the word (pause) **sing.** Say the sounds in **sing.** Get ready. (Signal for each sound as the children say) *sss* (pause) *ing.* (Repeat until firm.)

b. Everybody, write the word (pause) **sing.** ✓

c. (Repeat a and b for **sand, arm, salt, swim.**)

EXERCISE 3

Write cap, bed, fish, of, stop

a. You're going to write the word (pause) **cap.** Think about the sounds in **cap** and write the word. ✓

b. (Repeat a for **bed, fish, of, stop.**)

SENTENCE WRITING

EXERCISE 4

Write two sentences

a. Listen to this sentence. **He will run and fall.** Say that sentence. Get ready. (Signal.) *He will run and fall.*

---

b. Now you're going to say that sentence the slow way. Get ready. (Signal for each word as the children say) *He* (pause) *will* (pause) *run* (pause) *and* (pause) *fall.*

c. Everybody, write the sentence. Spell each word the right way. ✓

d. (Repeat a through c for **A ball fell in the mud.**)

END OF SPELLING LESSON 141

Lesson 142

SOUND WRITING

EXERCISE 1

Reinforce sound combination wh

a. (Write on the board: **wh.**)

b. (Point to **wh.**) Everybody, tell me the sound these letters make. Get ready. (Signal.) *whwhwh.* Yes, **whwhwh.**

c. (Erase **wh.**) Everybody, write the letters that go together and make the sound **wh.** ✓

WORD WRITING

EXERCISE 2

Write sound combination words where, when, what

a. (Write on the board: **where, when, what.**)

b. (Point to **where.**) Everybody, read this word the fast way. Get ready. (Signal.) *Where.* Yes, **where.** ✓

c. Everybody, say the sounds you write for the word (pause) **where.** Get ready. (Touch **wh, e, r, e** as the children say) *whwhwh* (pause) *eee* (pause) *rrr* (pause) *ēēē.* (Repeat until firm.)

d. (Erase **where.**) Everybody, write the word (pause) **where.** ✓

e. (Repeat *b* through *d* for **when, what.**)

Say the sounds, write **him, with, pill**

a. You're going to write the word (pause) **him.** Say the sounds in **him.** Get ready. (Signal for each sound as the children say) *h* (pause) *iii* (pause) *mmm.* (Repeat until firm.)

b. Everybody, write the word (pause) **him.** ✓

c. (Repeat *a* and *b* for **with, pill.**)

Write **fed, red, car, stop, also**

a. You're going to write the word (pause) **fed.** Think about the sounds in **fed** and write the word. ✓

b. (Repeat *a* for **red, car, stop, also.**)

SENTENCE WRITING

Write two sentences

a. Listen to this sentence. **His cap fell in the sand.** Say that sentence. Get ready. (Signal.) *His cap fell in the sand.*

b. Now you're going to say that sentence the slow way. Get ready. (Signal for each word as the children say) *His* (pause) *cap* (pause) *fell* (pause) *in* (pause) *the* (pause) *sand.*

c. Everybody, write the sentence. Spell each word the right way. ✓

d. (Repeat *a* through *c* for **This pig can run.**)

END OF SPELLING LESSON 142

Lesson 143

SOUND WRITING

Reinforce sound combination **wh**

a. (Write on the board: **wh.**)

b. (Point to **wh.**) Everybody, tell me the sound these letters make. Get ready. (Signal.) *whwhwh.* Yes, **whwhwh.**

c. (Erase **wh.**) Everybody, write the letters that go together and make the sound **wh.** ✓

WORD WRITING

Write sound combination words **when, where, what**

a. (Write on the board: **when, where, what.**)

b. (Point to **when.**) Everybody, read this word the fast way. Get ready. (Signal.) *When.* Yes, **when.**

c. Everybody, say the sounds you write for the word (pause) **when.** Get ready. (Touch **wh, e, n** as the children say) *whwhwh* (pause) *eee* (pause) *nnn.* (Repeat until firm.)

d. (Erase **when.**) Everybody, write the word (pause) **when.** ✓

e. (Repeat *b* through *d* for **where, what.**)

Say the sounds, write **thing, now, dish**

a. You're going to write the word (pause) **thing.** Say the sounds in **thing.** Get ready. (Signal for each sound as the children say) *th* (pause) *ing.* (Repeat until firm.)

b. Everybody, write the word (pause) **thing.** ✓

c. (Repeat *a* and *b* for **now, dish.**)

EXERCISE 4

Write **ten, sand, of, hen, bug, salt**

a. You're going to write the word (pause) **ten.** Think about the sounds in **ten** and write the word. ✓

b. (Repeat a for **sand, of, hen, bug, salt.**)

SENTENCE WRITING

EXERCISE 5

Write two sentences

a. Listen to this sentence. **The mop is on the rug.** Say that sentence. Get ready. (Signal.) *The mop is on the rug.*

b. Now you're going to say that sentence the slow way. Get ready. (Signal for each word as the children say) *The* (pause) *mop* (pause) *is* (pause) *on* (pause) *the* (pause) *rug.*

c. Everybody, write the sentence. Spell each word the right way. ✓

d. (Repeat a through c for **His dog has a bell.**)

END OF SPELLING LESSON 143

Lesson 144

SOUND WRITING

EXERCISE 1

Write **wh**

a. Everybody, you're going to write the letters that go together and make the sound **wh.** What sound? (Signal.) *whwhwh.*

b. Write **wh.** ✓

WORD WRITING

EXERCISE 2

Write sound combination words **when, what, where**

a. (Write on the board: **when, what, where.**)

b. (Point to **when.**) Everybody, read this word the fast way. Get ready. (Signal.) *When.* Yes, **when.**

c. Everybody, say the sounds you write for the word (pause) **when.** Get ready. (Touch **wh, e, n** as the children say) *whwhwh* (pause) *eee* (pause) *nnn.* (Repeat until firm.)

d. (Erase **when.**) Everybody, write the word (pause) **when.** ✓

e. (Repeat b through d for **what, where.**)

EXERCISE 3

Say the sounds, write **wish, hut, come, said**

a. You're going to write the word (pause) **wish.** Say the sounds in **wish.** Get ready. (Signal for each sound as the children say) *www* (pause) *iii* (pause) *shshsh.* (Repeat until firm.)

b. Everybody, write the word (pause) **wish.** ✓

c. (Repeat a and b for **hut, come, said.**)

EXERCISE 4

Write **bark, to, but, hill**

a. You're going to write the word (pause) **bark.** Think about the sounds in **bark** and write the word. ✓

b. (Repeat a for **to, but, hill.**)

SENTENCE WRITING

EXERCISE 5

Write two sentences

a. Listen to this sentence. **His pig can sing.** Say that sentence. Get ready. (Signal.) *His pig can sing.*

b. Now you're going to say that sentence the slow way. Get ready. (Signal for each word as the children say) *His* (pause) *pig* (pause) *can* (pause) *sing.*

c. Everybody, write the sentence. Spell each word the right way. ✓

d. (Repeat *a* through *c* for **That hen is not tall.**)

END OF SPELLING LESSON 144

Lesson 145

SOUND WRITING

Write wh

a. Everybody, you're going to write the letters that go together and make the sound **wh**. What sound? (Signal.) *wh.*

b. Write **wh**. ✓

WORD WRITING

Write sound combination words what, where, when

a. (Write on the board: **what, where, when.**)

b. (Point to **what.**) Everybody, read this word the fast way. Get ready. (Signal.) *What.* Yes, **what.**

c. Everybody, say the sounds you write for the word (pause) **what.** Get ready. (Touch **wh, a, t** as the children say) *wh* (pause) *aaa* (pause) *t.* (Repeat until firm.)

d. (Erase **what.**) Everybody, write the word (pause) **what.** ✓

e. (Repeat *b* through *d* for **where, when.**)

Write are

a. You're going to write the word (pause) **are.** What word? (Signal.) *Are.*

b. Everybody, write the word (pause) **are.** ✓

Say the sounds, write stop, if, ball

a. You're going to write the word (pause) **stop.** Say the sounds in **stop.** Get ready. (Signal for each sound as the children say) *sss* (pause) *t* (pause) *ooo* (pause) *p.* (Repeat until firm.)

b. Everybody, write the word (pause) **stop.** ✓

c. (Repeat *a* and *b* for **if, ball.**)

Write tall, cow, us, bus

a. You're going to write the word (pause) **tall.** Think about the sounds in **tall** and write the word. ✓

b. (Repeat *a* for **cow, us, bus.**)

SENTENCE WRITING

Write two sentences

a. Listen to this sentence. **She will sit with me.** Say that sentence. Get ready. (Signal.) *She will sit with me.*

b. Now you're going to say that sentence the slow way. Get ready. (Signal for each word as the children say) *She* (pause) *will* (pause) *sit* (pause) *with* (pause) *me.*

c. Everybody, write the sentence. Spell each word the right way. ✓

d. (Repeat *a* through *c* for **That hen is in the sun.**)

END OF SPELLING LESSON 145

Lesson 146

WORD WRITING

Write are

a. You're going to write the word (pause) **are.** What word? (Signal.) *Are.*

b. Everybody, write the word (pause) **are.** ✓

Say the sounds, write **barn, stop, went, what, where**

a. You're going to write the word (pause) **barn.** Say the sounds in **barn.** Get ready. (Signal for each sound as the children say) *b* (pause) *ar* (pause) *nnn.*
(Repeat until firm.)

b. Everybody, write the word (pause) **barn.** ✓

c. (Repeat *a* and *b* for **stop, went, what, where.**)

Write **far, hill, ship, cop, ring**

a. You're going to write the word (pause) **far.** Think about the sounds in **far** and write the word. ✓

b. (Repeat *a* for **hill, ship, cop, ring.**)

SENTENCE WRITING

Write two sentences

a. Listen to this sentence. **This ball is big.** Say that sentence. Get ready. (Signal.) *This ball is big.*

b. Now you're going to say that sentence the slow way. Get ready. (Signal for each word as the children say) *This* (pause) *ball* (pause) *is* (pause) *big.*

c. Everybody, write the sentence. Spell each word the right way. ✓

d. (Repeat *a* through *c* for **She did not call him.**)

END OF SPELLING LESSON 146

Lesson 147

WORD WRITING

Say the sounds, write **when, also, where, come**

a. You're going to write the word (pause) **when.** Say the sounds in **when.** Get ready. (Signal for each sound as the children say) *whwhwh* (pause) *eee* (pause) *nnn.*
(Repeat until firm.)

b. Everybody, write the word (pause) **when.** ✓

c. (Repeat *a* and *b* for **also, where, come.**)

Write **up, cup, sand, ham, met, wall**

a. You're going to write the word (pause) **up.** Think about the sounds in **up** and write the word. ✓

b. (Repeat *a* for **cup, sand, ham, met, wall.**)

SENTENCE WRITING

Write two sentences

a. Listen to this sentence. **His bell did not ring.** Say that sentence. Get ready. (Signal.) *His bell did not ring.*

b. Now you're going to say that sentence the slow way. Get ready. (Signal for each word as the children say) *His* (pause) *bell* (pause) *did* (pause) *not* (pause) *ring.*

c. Everybody, write the sentence. Spell each word the right way. ✓

d. (Repeat *a* through *c* for **This cow has a barn.**)

END OF SPELLING LESSON 147

Lesson 148

SOUND WRITING

Introduce sound combination **er**

a. (Write on the board: **er.**)

b. (Point to **er.**) Everybody, tell me the sound these letters make. Get ready. (Signal.) *er.* Yes, **er.**

c. (Erase **er.**) Everybody, write the letters that go together and make the sound **ur.** ✓

WORD WRITING

Say the sounds, write **stop, dug, salt, swim**

a. You're going to write the word (pause) **stop.** Say the sounds in **stop.** Get ready. (Signal for each sound as the children say) *sss* (pause) *t* (pause) *ooo* (pause) *p.* (Repeat until firm.)
b. Everybody, write the word (pause) **stop.** ✓
c. (Repeat *a* and *b* for **dug, salt, swim.**)

Write **are, cop, shop, what, then, park**

a. You're going to write the word (pause) **are.** Think about the sounds in **are** and write the word. ✓
b. (Repeat *a* for **cop, shop, what, then, park.**)

SENTENCE WRITING

Write two sentences

a. Listen to this sentence. **His dog has the ham.** Say that sentence. Get ready. (Signal.) *His dog has the ham.*
b. Now you're going to say that sentence the slow way. Get ready. (Signal for each word as the children say) *His* (pause) *dog* (pause) *has* (pause) *the* (pause) *ham.*
c. Everybody, write the sentence. Spell each word the right way. ✓
d. (Repeat *a* through *c* for **The pig ran up the hill.**)

END OF SPELLING LESSON 148

Lesson 149

SOUND WRITING

Reinforce sound combination **er**

a. (Write on the board: **er.**)
b. (Point to **er.**) Everybody, tell me the sound these letters make. Get ready. (Signal.) *er.* Yes, **er.**
c. (Erase **er.**) Everybody, write the letters that go together and make the sound **er.** ✓

WORD WRITING

Write sound combination words **ever, never, other, her**

a. (Write on the board: **ever, never, other, her.**)
b. (Point to **ever.**) Everybody, read this word the fast way. Get ready. (Signal.) *Ever.* Yes, **ever.**
c. Everybody, say the sounds you write for the word (pause) **ever.** Get ready. (Touch **e, v, er** as the children say) *eee* (pause) *vvv* (pause) *er.* (Repeat until firm.)
d. (Erase **ever.**) Everybody, write the word (pause) **ever.** ✓
e. (Repeat *b* through *d* for **never, other, her.**)

Say the sounds, write **how, do, with**

a. You're going to write the word (pause) **how.** Say the sounds in **how.** Get ready. (Signal for each sound as the children say) *h* (pause) *ooo* (pause) *www.* (Repeat until firm.)
b. Everybody, write the word (pause) **how.** ✓
c. (Repeat *a* and *b* for **do, with.**)

EXERCISE 4

Write **when, of, tell, fell, big**

a. You're going to write the word (pause) **when.** Think about the sounds in **when** and write the word. ✓

b. (Repeat *a* for **of, tell, fell, big.**)

SENTENCE WRITING

EXERCISE 5

Write two sentences

a. Listen to this sentence. **The man has the cup.** Say that sentence. Get ready. (Signal.) *The man has the cup.*

b. Now you're going to say that sentence the slow way. Get ready. (Signal for each word as the children say) *The* (pause) *man* (pause) *has* (pause) *the* (pause) *cup.*

c. Everybody, write the sentence. Spell each word the right way. ✓

d. (Repeat *a* through *c* for **A cow ran up the hill.**)

END OF SPELLING LESSON 149

Lesson 150

SOUND WRITING

EXERCISE 1

Reinforce sound combination **er**

a. (Write on the board: **er.**)

b. (Point to **er.**) Everybody, tell me the sound these letters make. Get ready. (Signal.) *er.* Yes, **er.**

c. (Erase **er.**) Everybody, write the letters that go together and make the sound **er.** ✓

WORD WRITING

EXERCISE 2

Write sound combination words **her, other, never**

a. (Write on the board: **her, other, never.**)

b. (Point to **her.**) Everybody, read this word the fast way. Get ready. (Signal.) *Her.* Yes, **her.**

c. Everybody, say the sounds you write for the word (pause) **her.** Get ready. (Touch **h, er** as the children say) *h* (pause) *er.* (Repeat until firm.)

d. (Erase **her.**) Everybody, write the word (pause) **her.** ✓

e. (Point to **other.**) Everybody, read this word the fast way. Get ready. (Signal.) *Other.* Yes, **other.**

f. Everybody, say the sounds you write for the word (pause) **other.** Get ready. (Touch **o, th, er** as the children say) *ooo* (pause) *ththth* (pause) *er.* (Repeat until firm.)

g. (Erase **other.**) Everybody, write the word (pause) **other.** ✓

h. (Repeat *e* through *g* for **never.**)

EXERCISE 3

Say the sounds, write **what, sell, had**

a. You're going to write the word (pause) **what.** Say the sounds in **what.** Get ready. (Signal for each sound as the children say) *whwhwh* (pause) *aaa* (pause) *t.* (Repeat until firm.)

b. Everybody, write the word (pause) **what.** ✓

c. (Repeat *a* and *b* for **sell, had.**)

EXERCISE 4

Write **it, hit, fit, top, men, at**

a. You're going to write the word (pause) **it.** Think about the sounds in **it** and write the word. ✓

b. (Repeat *a* for **hit, fit, top, men, at.**)

SENTENCE WRITING

Write two sentences

a. Listen to this sentence. **That fish will get fat.** Say that sentence. Get ready. (Signal.) *That fish will get fat.*

b. Now you're going to say that sentence the slow way. Get ready. (Signal for each word as the children say) *That* (pause) *fish* (pause) *will* (pause) *get* (pause) *fat.*

c. Everybody, write the sentence. Spell each word the right way. ✓

d. (Repeat *a* through *c* for **His dog can run and bark.**)

END OF SPELLING LESSON 150

Lesson 151

SOUND WRITING

EXERCISE 1

Write er

a. Everybody, you're going to write the letters that go together and make the sound **er.** What sound? (Signal.) *er.*

b. Write **er.** ✓

WORD WRITING

EXERCISE 2

Write sound combination words never, other, ever, her

a. (Write on the board: **never, other, ever, her.**)

b. (Point to **never.**) Everybody, read this word the fast way. Get ready. (Signal.) *Never.* Yes, **never.**

c. Everybody, say the sounds you write for the word (pause) **never.** Get ready. (Touch **n, e, v, er** as the children say) *nnn* (pause) *eee* (pause) *vvv* (pause) *er.*
(Repeat until firm.)

d. (Erase **never.**) Everybody, write the word (pause) **never.** ✓

e. (Repeat *b* through *d* for **other, ever, her.**)

EXERCISE 3

Say the sounds, write pet, shot, got

a. You're going to write the word (pause) **pet.** Say the sounds in **pet.** Get ready. (Signal for each sound as the children say) *p* (pause) *eee* (pause) *t.*
(Repeat until firm.)

b. Everybody, write the word (pause) **pet.** ✓

c. (Repeat *a* and *b* for **shot, got.**)

EXERCISE 4

Write pit, had, when, farm

a. You're going to write the word (pause) **pit.** Think about the sounds in **pit** and write the word. ✓

b. (Repeat *a* for **had, when, farm.**)

SENTENCE WRITING

EXERCISE 5

Write two sentences

a. Listen to this sentence. **We did not get wet.** Say that sentence. Get ready. (Signal.) *We did not get wet.*

b. Now you're going to say that sentence the slow way. Get ready. (Signal for each word as the children say) *We* (pause) *did* (pause) *not* (pause) *get* (pause) *wet.*

c. Everybody, write the sentence. Spell each word the right way. ✓

d. (Repeat *a* through *c* for **She has a dog and a cat.**)

END OF SPELLING LESSON 151

Lesson 152

SOUND WRITING

EXERCISE 1

Write er

a. Everybody, you're going to write the letters that go together and make the sound **er.** What sound? (Signal.) *er.*
b. Write **er.** ✓

WORD WRITING

EXERCISE 2

Write sound combination words ever, other, her, never

a. (Write on the board: **ever, other, her, never.**)
b. (Point to **ever.**) Everybody, read this word the fast way. Get ready. (Signal.) *Ever.* Yes, **ever.**
c. Everybody, say the sounds you write for the word (pause) **ever.** Get ready. (Touch **e, v, er** as the children say) *eee* (pause) *vvv* (pause) *er.* (Repeat until firm.)
d. (Erase **ever.**) Everybody, write the word (pause) **ever.** ✓
e. (Repeat *b* through *d* for **other, her, never.**)

EXERCISE 3

Say the sounds, write thing, got, wish, where

a. You're going to write the word (pause) **thing.** Say the sounds in **thing.** Get ready. (Signal for each sound as the children say) *thththth* (pause) *ing.* (Repeat until firm.)
b. Everybody, write the word (pause) **thing.** ✓
c. (Repeat *a* and *b* for **got, wish, where.**)

EXERCISE 4

Write shot, salt, went, get, is

a. You're going to write the word (pause) **shot.** Think about the sounds in **shot** and write the word. ✓
b. (Repeat *a* for **salt, went, get, is.**)

SENTENCE WRITING

EXERCISE 5

Write two sentences

a. Listen to this sentence. **He has a nut and a cat.** Say that sentence. Get ready. (Signal.) *He has a nut and a cat.*
b. Now you're going to say that sentence the slow way. Get ready. (Signal for each word as the children say) *He* (pause) *has* (pause) *a* (pause) *nut* (pause) *and* (pause) *a* (pause) *cat.*
c. Everybody, write the sentence. Spell each word the right way. ✓
d. (Repeat *a* through *c* for **We are on a farm.**)

END OF SPELLING LESSON 152

Lesson 153

WORD WRITING

EXERCISE 1

Say the sounds, write other, card, leg, beg

a. You're going to write the word (pause) **other.** Say the sounds in **other.** Get ready. (Signal for each sound as the children say) *ooo* (pause) *th* (pause) *er.*
(Repeat until firm.)
b. Everybody, write the word (pause) **other.** ✓
c. (Repeat *a* and *b* for **card, leg, beg.**)

EXERCISE 2

Write her, what, up, where, come, with, also

a. You're going to write the word (pause) **her.** Think about the sounds in **her** and write the word. ✓
b. (Repeat *a* for **what, up, where, come, with, also.**)

SENTENCE WRITING

EXERCISE 3

Write two sentences

a. Listen to this sentence. **She has a hat and a rat.** Say that sentence. Get ready. (Signal.) *She has a hat and a rat.*

b. Now you're going to say that sentence the slow way. Get ready. (Signal for each word as the children say) *She* (pause) *has* (pause) *a* (pause) *hat* (pause) *and* (pause) *a* (pause) *rat.*

c. Everybody, write the sentence. Spell each word the right way. ✓

d. (Repeat *a* through *c* for **We are on the ship.**)

END OF SPELLING LESSON 153

Lesson 154

WORD WRITING

EXERCISE 1

Say the sounds, write ring, leg, said, other, brother

a. You're going to write the word (pause) **ring.** Say the sounds in **ring.** Get ready. (Signal for each sound as the children say) *rrr* (pause) *ing.* (Repeat until firm.)

b. Everybody, write the word (pause) **ring.** ✓

c. (Repeat *a* and *b* for **leg, said, other, brother.**)

EXERCISE 2

Write when, what, shot, met, got, them

a. You're going to write the word (pause) **when.** Think about the sounds in **when** and write the word. ✓

b. (Repeat *a* for **what, shot, met, got, them.**)

SENTENCE WRITING

EXERCISE 3

Write three sentences

a. Listen to this sentence. **That bus will not stop.** Say that sentence. Get ready. (Signal.) *That bus will not stop.*

b. Now you're going to say that sentence the slow way. Get ready. (Signal for each word as the children say) *That* (pause) *bus* (pause) *will* (pause) *not* (pause) *stop.*

c. Everybody, write the sentence. Spell each word the right way. ✓

d. (Repeat *a* through *c* for **The men are sad** and **She has a dog.**)

END OF SPELLING LESSON 154

Lesson 155

SOUND WRITING

EXERCISE 1

Introduce sound combination ck

a. (Write on the board: **ck.**)

b. (Point to **ck.**) Everybody, tell me the sound these letters make. Get ready. (Signal.) *k.* Yes, **k.**

c. (Erase **ck.**) Everybody, write the letters that go together and make the sound **k.** ✓

WORD WRITING

EXERCISE 2

Say the sounds, write rug, bug, brother, ever

a. You're going to write the word (pause) **rug.** Say the sounds in **rug.** Get ready. (Signal for each sound as the children say) *rrr* (pause) *uuu* (pause) *g.* (Repeat until firm.)

b. Everybody, write the word (pause) **rug.** ✓

c. (Repeat *a* and *b* for **bug, brother, ever.**)

Write **where, shot, beg, top, cop, other**

a. You're going to write the word (pause) **where.** Think about the sounds in **where** and write the word. ✓

b. (Repeat a for **shot, beg, top, cop, other.**)

SENTENCE WRITING

EXERCISE 4

Write three sentences

a. Listen to this sentence. **His car will not run.** Say that sentence. Get ready. (Signal.) *His car will not run.*

b. Now you're going to say that sentence the slow way. Get ready. (Signal for each word as the children say) *His* (pause) *car* (pause) *will* (pause) *not* (pause) *run.*

c. Everybody, write the sentence. Spell each word the right way. ✓

d. (Repeat a through c for **She did not fall** and **Her dog is fat.**)

END OF SPELLING LESSON 155

Lesson 156

SOUND WRITING

EXERCISE 1

Reinforce sound combination **ck**

a. (Write on the board: **ck.**)

b. (Point to **ck.**) Everybody, tell me the sound these letters make. Get ready. (Signal.) *k.* Yes, **k.**

c. (Erase **ck.**) Everybody, write the letters that go together and make the sound **k.** ✓

WORD WRITING

EXERCISE 2

Write sound combination words **pack, back, rock, sock**

a. (Write on the board: **pack, back, rock, sock.**)

b. (Point to **pack.**) Everybody, read this word the fast way. Get ready. (Signal.) *Pack.* Yes, **pack.**

c. Everybody, say the sounds you write for the word (pause) **pack.** Get ready. (Touch **p, a, ck** as the children say) *p* (pause) *aaa* (pause) *k.* (Repeat until firm.)

d. (Erase **pack.**) Everybody, write the word (pause) **pack.** ✓

e. (Repeat b through d for **back, rock, sock.**)

WORD WRITING

EXERCISE 3

Say the sounds, write **never, after, also, other, mother**

a. You're going to write the word (pause) **never.** Say the sounds in **never.** Get ready. (Signal for each sound as the children say) *nnn* (pause) *eee* (pause) *vvv* (pause) *er.* (Repeat until firm.)

b. Everybody, write the word (pause) **never.** ✓

c. (Repeat a and b for **after, also, other, mother.**)

EXERCISE 4

Write **to, what, arm, when, brother, had**

a. You're going to write the word (pause) **to.** Think about the sounds in **to** and write the word. ✓

b. (Repeat a for **what, arm, when, brother, had.**)

SENTENCE WRITING

EXERCISE 5

Write three sentences

a. Listen to this sentence. **That cop can sing.** Say that sentence. Get ready. (Signal.) *That cop can sing.*

b. Now you're going to say that sentence the slow way. Get ready. (Signal for each word as the children say) *That* (pause) *cop* (pause) *can* (pause) *sing.*
c. Everybody, write the sentence. Spell each word the right way. ✓
d. (Repeat *a* through *c* for **He did not hit her** and **She has a fish.**)

END OF SPELLING LESSON 156

Lesson 157

SOUND WRITING

| EXERCISE 1 |

Reinforce sound combination ck

a. (Write on the board: **ck.**)
b. (Point to **ck.**) Everybody, tell me the sound these letters make. Get ready. (Signal.) *k.* Yes, **k.**
c. (Erase **ck.**) Everybody, write the letters that go together and make the sound **k.** ✓

WORD WRITING

| EXERCISE 2 |

Write sound combination words rock, sock, sack, pick

a. (Write on the board: **rock, sock, sack, pick.**)

---

b. (Point to **rock.**) Everybody, read this word the fast way. Get ready. (Signal.) *Rock.* Yes, **rock.**
c. Everybody, say the sounds you write for the word (pause) **rock.** Get ready. (Touch **r, o, ck** as the children say) *rrr* (pause) *ooo* (pause) *k.* (Repeat until firm.)
d. (Erase **rock.**) Everybody, write the word (pause) **rock.** ✓
e. (Repeat *b* through *d* for **sock, sack, pick.**)

WORD WRITING

| EXERCISE 3 |

Write him, with, went, fun, got, after, tall, cow

a. You're going to write the word (pause) **him.** Think about the sounds in **him** and write the word. ✓
b. (Repeat *a* for **with, went, fun, got, after, tall, cow.**)

SENTENCE WRITING

| EXERCISE 4 |

Write three sentences

a. Listen to this sentence. **We will never run.** Say that sentence. Get ready. (Signal.) *We will never run.*

---

b. Now you're going to say that sentence the slow way. Get ready. (Signal for each word as the children say) *We* (pause) *will* (pause) *never* (pause) *run.*
c. Everybody, write the sentence. Spell each word the right way. ✓
d. (Repeat *a* through *c* for **He can hop and sing** and **We are on the ship.**)

END OF SPELLING LESSON 157

Lesson 158

SOUND WRITING

| EXERCISE 1 |

Reinforce sound combination ck

a. (Write on the board: **ck.**)
b. (Point to **ck.**) Everybody, tell me the sound these letters make. Get ready. (Signal.) *k.* Yes, **k.**
c. Erase **ck.** Everybody, write the letters that go together and make the sound **k.** ✓

WORD WRITING

| EXERCISE 2 |

Write sound combination words pack, rock, sock, back

a. Write on the board: **pack, rock, sock, back.**

b. Point to **pack.** Everybody, read this word the fast way. Get ready. (Signal.) *Pack.* Yes, **pack.**

c. Everybody, say the sounds you write for the word (pause) **pack.** Get ready. (Touch **p, a, ck** as the children say) *p* (pause) *aaa* (pause) *k.* (Repeat until firm.)

d. Erase **pack.** Everybody, write the word (pause) **pack.** ✓

e. Repeat *b* through *d* for **rock, sock, back.**

WORD WRITING

Say the sounds, write her, rock, pack, where, has, mother

a. You're going to write the word (pause) **her.** Say the sounds in **her.** Get ready. (Signal for each sound as the children say) *h* (pause) *er.* (Repeat until firm.)

b. Everybody, write the word (pause) **her.** ✓

c. (Repeat *a* and *b* for **rock, pack, where, has, mother.**)

Write bark, stop, ever, sing, of, dish

a. You're going to write the word (pause) **bark.** Think about the sounds in **bark** and write the word. ✓

b. (Repeat *a* for **stop, ever, sing, of, dish.**)

SENTENCE WRITING

Write three sentences

a. Listen to this sentence. **That man went with him.** Say that sentence. Get ready. (Signal.) *That man went with him.*

b. Now you're going to say that sentence the slow way. Get ready. (Signal for each word as the children say) *That* (pause) *man* (pause) *went* (pause) *with* (pause) *him.*

c. Everybody, write the sentence. Spell each word the right way. ✓

d. (Repeat *a* through *c* for **The men are in the barn** and **He has a ball.**)

END OF SPELLING LESSON 158

Lesson 159

SOUND WRITING

Reinforce sound combination ck

a. (Write on the board: **ck.**)

b. (Point to **ck.**) Everybody, tell me the sound these letters make. Get ready. (Signal.) *k.* Yes, **k.**

c. (Erase **ck.**) Everybody, write the letters that go together and make the sound **k.** ✓

WORD WRITING

Write sound combination words pack, back, rock, sock

a. (Write on the board: **pack, back, rock, sock.**)

b. (Point to **pack.**) Everybody, read this word the fast way. Get ready. (Signal.) *Pack.* Yes, **pack.**

c. Everybody, say the sounds you write for the word (pause) **pack.** Get ready. (Touch **p, a, ck** as the children say) *p* (pause) *aaa* (pause) *k.* (Repeat until firm.)

d. (Erase **pack.**) Everybody, write the word (pause) **pack.** ✓

e. (Repeat *b* through *d* for **back, rock, sock.**)

WORD WRITING

Say the sounds, write hand, when, ship

a. You're going to write the word (pause) **hand.** Say the sounds in **hand.** Get ready. (Signal for each sound as the children say) *h* (pause) *aaa* (pause) *nnn* (pause) *d.* (Repeat until firm.)

b. Everybody, write the word (pause) **hand.** ✓

c. (Repeat *a* and *b* for **when, ship.**)

EXERCISE 4

Write **top, hop, cop, swim, other, brother, card, if**

a. You're going to write the word (pause) **top.** Think about the sounds in **top** and write the word. ✓

b. (Repeat *a* for **hop, cop, swim, other, brother, card, if.**)

SENTENCE WRITING

EXERCISE 5

Write three sentences

a. Listen to this sentence. **That ham is on the dish.** Say that sentence. Get ready. (Signal.) *That ham is on the dish.*

b. Now you're going to say that sentence the slow way. Get ready. (Signal for each word as the children say) *That* (pause) *ham* (pause) *is* (pause) *on* (pause) *the* (pause) *dish.*

c. Everybody, write the sentence. Spell each word the right way. ✓

d. (Repeat *a* through *c* for **This dog can dig** and **She went with him.**)

END OF SPELLING LESSON 159

Lesson 160

WORD WRITING

EXERCISE 1

Write sound combination words **rock, sock, sack, pick**

a. (Write on the board: **rock, sock, sack,** and **pick.**)

b. (Point to **rock.**) Everybody, read this word the fast way. Get ready. (Signal.) *Rock.* Yes, **rock.**

c. Everybody, say the sounds you write for the word (pause) **rock.** Get ready. (Touch **r, o, ck** as the children say) *rrr* (pause) *ooo* (pause) *k.* (Repeat until firm.)

d. (Erase **rock.**) Everybody, write the word (pause) **rock.** ✓

e. (Repeat *b* through *d* for **sock, sack, pick.**)

EXERCISE 2

Say the sounds, write **sock, back, pack**

a. You're going to write the word (pause) **sock.** Say the sounds in **sock.** Get ready. (Signal for each sound as the children say) *sss* (pause) *ooo* (pause) *k.* (Repeat until firm.)

b. Everybody, write the word (pause) **sock.** ✓

c. (Repeat *a* and *b* for **back, pack.**)

EXERCISE 3

Write **brother, mother, wall, call, how, where**

a. You're going to write the word (pause) **brother.** Think about the sounds in **brother** and write the word. ✓

b. (Repeat *a* for **mother, wall, call, how, where.**)

SENTENCE WRITING

EXERCISE 4

Write three sentences

a. Listen to this sentence. **A hen can not bark.** Say that sentence. Get ready. (Signal.) *A hen can not bark.*

b. Now you're going to say that sentence the slow way. Get ready. (Signal for each word as the children say) *A* (pause) *hen* (pause) *can* (pause) *not* (pause) *bark.*

c. Everybody, write the sentence. Spell each word the right way. ✓

d. (Repeat *a* through *c* for **He went with her** and **That rock is in the sand.**)

END OF SPELLING LESSON 160